FISHER'S
LAWS

FISHER'S LAWS

The Thinker's Guide to Management Action

WILLIAM P. FISHER, PH.D.

LEBHAR-FRIEDMAN BOOKS

NEW YORK CHICAGO LOS ANGELES LONDON PARIS TOKYO

Lebhar-Friedman Books
425 Park Avenue
New York, NY 10022

Published by Lebhar-Friedman Books
Lebhar-Friedman Books is a company of Lebhar-Friedman Inc.

Printed in the United States of America

Library of Congress Cataloging-in-Publication Data
Fisher, William P.
   Fisher's laws: the thinker's guide to management action / William P.
Fisher.
       p.   cm.
   Includes index.
   ISBN 0-86730-786-2
   1. Leadership. 2. Management. 3. Decision making. I. Title.
HD57.7.F58   2000
658.4'092–dc21   99-30507
                                                              CIP

Design by Merri Ann Morrell

Visit our Web site at lfbooks.com.

Volume Discounts
This book makes a great gift and incentive.
Call (212) 756-5240 for information on volume discounts.

This book is dedicated to my beautiful wife of thirty-five years, Yvonne; our three children, Suzanne Fisher Boyer, Michael W. Fisher, and Thomas C. Fisher; our son-in-law, Stephen P. Boyer; our daughter-in-law, Amy Beth Fisher; and our four grandchildren, Kathryn Grace Boyer, Courtney Elizabeth Boyer, John William Boyer, and William Thomas Fisher. They are the inspiration for my life.

CONTENTS

CONTENTS

PREFACE

In numerous conversations with executives at all levels of management in different fields of endeavor, I have heard a common lament that goes something like this: "Where can I find a practical book on management that tells it like it is rather than espousing some management theory that happens to be the latest fad in organizational literature?" Perhaps you have had the same thought without necessarily expressing it to someone else.

In the past few years, the subjects of leadership and management have come under intense scrutiny, as many people believe there is a paucity of strong leaders and farsighted, effective managers in the various walks of life.

In preparation for a talk I was asked to give recently, I undertook a review of the literature to determine the state of the art on leadership and management as it's described through the printed word.

I found very little hard-hitting "hands-on" material that captured the heartbeat of everyday organizational functioning from a managerial perspective. Yes, there are a number of theories, models, approaches, charts, and opinions full of "You should . . ." and "It's recommended that . . ." I found very little "Here's the situation, here's what you need to think about, and what you have to consider before taking action."

Having a limited tolerance for theory and an unsatisfied hunger for a "meaty" book that is valuable to anyone in a managerial role, I decided to set my thoughts down on paper (okay, keyed them into the computer), having experienced most of what is contained herein.

More important, I hope that you will find the contents to be thought-provoking and beneficial.

The ultimate purpose of this book is to make you a better leader, a better manager, a better thinker, a better activator, and a better "boss."

Preface

I want to thank my valued and valuable assistant, Lou Ann Hill, for her ideas, support, suggested phraseology from time to time, and putting up with my changes of mind.

Happy reading!

William P. Fisher, Ph.D.
McLean, Virginia

FISHER'S
LAWS

1

EMBARKATION

As most people know, the profession of "management" is part art and part science. Successful management is as much a function of the values, habits, propensities, and style that emanate from within the manager (art) as it is a function of learning and practicing tried-and-true principles that are generally and universally accepted as eternal verities (science). Attitude is an example of the former, while the intertwining of responsibility and authority is an example of the latter.

Whether you are just starting out in the management ranks, are somewhere along the way in your management career, or are a seasoned veteran of managerial "wars" (with the scars to prove it), you can exercise your improvement attitude by contemplating the "laws" that comprise this volume.

The insights contained herein are as equally applicable to mentors as mentees, trainers as trainees, senior-level managers as junior-level managers. They are also equally applicable to any type or size of organization; for-profit, nonprofit, private sector, public sector, service industry, or manufacturing. Let's begin.

Wherever you are in whatever kind of organization, indelibly ingest **Fisher's Law #1.** It comes in two parts.

A. **Put your heart in your organization and your organization in your heart.**

B. **Keep your mind on your assignment and keep your assignment on your mind.**

2

CLIMBING AN ORGANIZATIONAL MOUNTAIN

As you proceed with your career, realize that there is a striking parallel between climbing an organizational mountain and climbing a terrestrial mountain.

If you intend to reach the summit, you must plan carefully, prepare well, secure the best equipment possible, know how and when to use that equipment, and surround yourself with other expert climbers. You must train both physically and mentally and seek advice from others who have made the climb before you. You'll need to maintain that single-mindedness of purpose, that the apex is the ultimate goal. History rarely recognizes organizational mountain climbers who are satisfied with scaling only half a mountain.

When starting out, you cannot be profligate with your resources or you'll not have them when you need them. You cannot be reckless or careless at lower levels or you will be doomed scarcely before you start, and you don't want a reputation of being a wastrel.

You need to follow your basic plan. Once initiated, your climb should be doggedly progressive, not wavering for loss of spirit or stamina. As you ascend the organizational mountain, the air becomes thinner and you will not cover the distance at higher levels that you did earlier within comparable time frames. Higher elevations give you a better view, but they require greater surety of movement. You've got to be in shape! The atmosphere gets colder, the ground can become slippery, and storms do occur. You will need some insulation, but it can't be so tight that it cuts off circulation. Thick skin helps!

At the higher levels, each additional step has to be considered carefully before it is taken. The safety line to the fall-back position must be absolutely secure. Risks will be encountered, and the unexpected will happen. Don't be immobilized by it. You can overcome unsettling occurrences using your resourcefulness and creativity. You must realize that you and others in your climbing party are interdependent.

As you continue your ascent, the details of lower altitudes lose focus because of sheer distance. You must expect that and cannot lament it. You should not step upward while looking downward, or your balance will be in jeopardy. Still, you must be mindful of the conditions below you.

At the highest elevations, the view is exhilarating and the sense of accomplishment is momentous. Never forget, however, that it takes one set of talents to get to the top, but some additional talents and resources are needed to remain there for any period of time. You may also feel a bit isolated from time to time, but that's the price you pay for your abilities. At some point you will leave the summit. It's just a question of whether you will step aside, step down, or fall down.

It's time for **Fisher's Law #2.**

If you are going to climb an organizational mountain, you've got to know the ropes!

3

MANAGEMENT ABC'S

Management is at once simple and complex. It's simple in concept, complex in conduct. Let's talk about the easy side first. I refer to these virtues as the management ABC's. There is such a thing as alphabet management, which is what you want to develop. Then again, there is the "malphabet" management, which, unfortunately, a lot of unsuccessful managers have developed. Here they both are:

Alphabet Management

ATTITUDE–it all starts here. Get a good one and never let it go!

BRIGHTNESS–covers both mental ability and personality. Sparkle!

COMPETENCE–it's the name of the game. Go for it!

DECISIVENESS–leaders act and don't look back!

EFFECTIVENESS–making an impact means making a difference!

FLEXIBILITY–if you can't bend, you'll snap!

GLIBNESS–one who speaks well sells well. You're always selling!

HONESTY–by definition, any deviance from total honesty is some degree of dishonesty!

INNOVATIVE–create creativity creatively!

JUDGMENT–call 'em like you see 'em, but be sure you see 'em!

KNOWLEDGEABLE–know the organization, know the industry, know yourself!

LOYALTY–it runs down as well as up!

METHODICAL–remember the tortoise and the hare?

NOBLE–if it's the right thing to do, do it right!

OBJECTIVITY–think with your mind, not your heart!

PRODUCTIVITY–produce productivity productively!

QUALITY-MINDEDNESS–this gives definition to your existence!

RESILIENT–no matter how hard the hit, you can come back!

SENSITIVITY–you're part of the world, not the center of it!

TENACITY–determined dedication for the best decisions!

UNDERSTANDING–mistakes will be made but should not be repeated!

VISION–it goes beyond "mission," it's organizational self-actualization!

WISDOM–intelligence supported by experience, ethics, and a moral core!

XENOPHILIC–openness to others is the essence of graciousness!

YEASTY–the best way to rise is to keep the organization rising!

ZEAL–be twice as good as yesterday, half as good as tomorrow!

These are some of the vices you want to avoid. They are career killers.

Malphabet Management

ARROGANCE–life is to serve others, not humble them!

BELLIGERENCE–if you're going to fight, be prepared to lose!

CRUDITY–is the pits, and that's where it belongs!

DECEPTION–if you lose your trustworthiness, nothing's left!

EGOCENTRICITY–you can't fool those who work for you!

FATUOUS–no one suffers fools very long!

GARRULOUS–talks a lot and says nothing!

HOSTILE–if people grate you, you'll never be great!

INEFFICIENT–waste hastens you out!

JEALOUSY–too bad self-improvement is subordinate to covetousness!

KLUTZY–insensitivity breeds contempt!

LAZINESS–remember the hare and the tortoise?

MALEVOLENT–one who is destructive cultivates destructiveness!

NEGLIGENT–if you overlook standards, you'll be overrun!

OPPRESSIVE–do you really think you're here to hold others back?

PETTINESS–is an anchor on progress!

QUARRELSOME–arguments usually shed more heat than light!

RESENTFUL–life can be unfair, but everyone gets a share of unfairness!

SPITEFUL–an eye for an eye makes you both half blind!

TEMPERAMENTAL–others will brood if you have changing moods!

UNCERTAINTY–indecision reflects insecurity!

VINDICTIVENESS–revenge is not becoming, it's debasing!

WAILING–crying doesn't solve the problem!

XENOPHOBIC–if you don't like people, there's always Mt. Everest!

YAHOO–we can all stand a little more polish and sophistication!

ZANY–there is a difference between being "off the plan" and "off the wall"!

Summing up, we have **Fisher's Law #3.**

Know your management ABC's!

4

REAL-WORLD
EDUCATION

I have found that next to the disciplines of finance and marketing, which are nine-tenths mechanics and one-tenth judgment, the most misunderstood discipline in organizational life is employee development. There are a lot of buzzwords in that realm that give rise to confusion and inarticulation. There are training programs, internships, development programs, educational programs, empowerment programs, and scores of other pious-sounding words and phrases, but you need to get behind the words to understand the concept.

Here's **Fisher's Law #4.**

> **Education is learning to think; training is learning to execute!**

That's an interesting distinction, and I'll give you an illustration.

You can train a dog, for example, to bark, shake hands, roll over, jump up, lie down, and perform any number of other tricks. The dog *does* something by *executing* on command. No one, however, would say the dog is educated. They may say the dog is smart, but we don't educate animals, we train them. Conversely, you have and will continue to receive an education, for education is a life-long process. Education is the process of intellectual development brought about by the infusion of knowledge, analytical skills, creativity skills, and problem-solving techniques. It's the internalization of knowledge, experience, and observation for use at an appropriate time. Education is more than training, for training does not necessarily require thought. Reflexes, yes! But not thought!

The point is that you need to be both a thinker and a doer, and moreover, you need to surround yourself with subordinates who are thinking doers. You can't be just one or the other and expect to be upwardly mobile and successful in your career over the long term.

You also need to understand two more points. One is **Fisher's Law #5.**

There is a difference between intelligence and education. A lot of intelligent people don't have an education, and vice versa. Measure yourself and others on intellectual merit, not educational credentials.

Now to the final point, with respect to education. It's expressed best as **Fisher's Law #6.**

Graduation ceremonies at schools are called "commencement." They are not called "conclusions."

Your real-world education is under way as you apply what you learned in school, and you'll also want to make every day a new learning experience. Education is a process, not a product.

5

ESSENTIALLY YOURS

Let me ask you a fundamental question, the answer to which will evoke your basic management philosophy and behavior as perceived by your subordinates.

Which position is the most important of these three: the manager, the manager's secretary, or the mailroom attendant?

No, this is not an intellectual trap. I suspect you are going to say they are all equally important.

If you do respond in that manner, you may be some sort of an idealist, or perhaps you just finished some sort of human relations seminar. If you don't have a sense of reality, you may want to reconsider your career options.

On the other hand, one could argue that the manager is the most important, as that position carries the greatest amount of responsibility. After all, organizations are, in fact, hierarchical structures.

But then again, are you going to tell the people in the mailroom that their positions are not as important as the secretary or the manager? Suppose everything stopped in the mailroom? How effective would the secretary and the manager be then? Or suppose the secretary stopped completing assigned duties? You can imagine what happens when you have these types of breakdowns.

Let's escape this conundrum with **Fisher's Law #7.**

Don't answer impossible questions.

Instead, articulate the real management concept that is being called forth in this example. I'll explain.

There is no question that there are different levels of responsibility, authority, reward systems, sanctions, and restrictions in any organization in terms of the requirements and scope of different positions. A manager's position is at a higher level than a secretary's, and so on. On the other hand, each job incumbent must perform as prescribed, or the entire organization suffers. Each position, therefore, is essential to and interdependent on all the others, due to its integration into the overall system. If a position is not essential, abolish it. You're wasting resources if you don't!

Let's sharpen our thinking, and we will all be the better off for it. **Fisher's Law #8 states:**

Communicate the essential nature of their positions to your subordinates, both in terms of the requirement for peak performance and in terms of their role in the overall organizational structure!

Not only do you need to tell them, but you need to show them by way of your own relationships with them, and in terms of your own conduct. You need to make them feel their own essentiality.

6

CONSISTENTLY YOURS

I want to tell you about an imaginary executive colleague of mine. We'll call this executive Elbaulav.

When Elbaulav first joined the organization, there was no training program. Consequently, no one was well prepared for his or her job. People sort of did their own thing, and it was haphazard at best, counterproductive at worst. Since Elbaulav had no training, performance was not good, but since the organization still had to function, errors were either overlooked or remedied by others before they became too serious.

Employees came and went, but Elbaulav stayed and was eventually promoted to department head on the basis of tenure. Elbaulav always made wrong decisions on business matters, but times were good and the organization seemed to succeed in spite of itself. Moreover, at staff meetings, Elbaulav always seemed to be advocating approaches or courses of action that the organization wound up not pursuing.

One day, the chief executive officer promoted Elbaulav to be his personal assistant. Whenever the CEO was faced with a crucial decision, he would turn to Elbaulav for advice and counsel. The CEO would then do the *exact opposite* of what Elbaulav recommended, and the organization became enormously successful. Elbaulav became the most valuable person ever employed by the organization, as people could count on Elbaulav *always being wrong*. My point can be summed up in **Fisher's Law #9.**

Consistency can often be as valuable as accuracy!

Just think about it for a moment. Accountants are guided by consistency. Advertising needs to be consistent to be effective. The application of human resources policies needs to be consistent, as does the execution of training programs.

What you may be thinking now is that this example somehow cheapens the value of accuracy.

Not so! Consider **Fisher's Law #10.**

Accuracy is paramount, but you *also* need to look for consistency!

While we're at it, let me say a word to you about "policy." It's **Fisher's Law #11.**

A policy is not a regulation. Policies are guideposts, not edicts. Apply them as appropriate but make exceptions when it's the right thing for the organization to do!

7

OBSESSION VS. COMPULSION

Allow me to ask about your basic philosophy. What is your immediate reaction when I say the word "work"? Is it positive in that it excites you? Do you feel properly challenged and stimulated? Is it a negative reaction in that you mentally wince when you hear it, and shy away from it, or consider it drudgery? I don't expect you to reveal your innermost thoughts, but I raise the question to make a point.

If one adopts, as part of a personal and professional philosophy, an attitude that work is there to be done, or if you can make it fun and can cause progress, it's better than considering work a necessary burden or an interruption to the rest of your life.

But that's only half of it. Attitude is the core foundation of every aspect of life, so it's important that you plant and cultivate a good one, as that will serve you well in whatever you do. Let me issue **Fisher's Law #12.**

> **Work is what you *get* to do, not what you *have* to do. Go after it and get it. Don't let it elude you!**

Now, the other half deals with the people you will be working with, for everyone doesn't have a positive attitude and a productive philosophy. It's a sad fact of life, but nonetheless, it is still a fact. If you hope to manage people or are currently managing them, you need to recognize this to still get maximum performance from them. That's an essential covenant of skillful management.

Take to heart **Fisher's Law #13.**

People work regardless of whether they do it to survive or because it is their philosophy of life to work or to maintain a certain lifestyle. The distinction between obsession and compulsion is not always obvious. It does not matter: Draw the most, and the best, from each of your employees.

It's up to you to set the conditions that cause people to *want* to work for you. Allow them to work out of inspiration, not perspiration.

Let me sum up with a two-part truism that serves as **Fisher's Law #14:**

A. Nothing succeeds like managerial success.

B. But the reciprocal is also true. Nothing fails like management failure.

8

AUTHORITY! RESPONSIBILITY!

It's time now to focus on two fundamental management concepts, **authority** and **responsibility,** and the relationship that exists between them.

The word **authority** has numerous meanings, among which are:

1. what one has as an expert in one's field
2. truthfulness, as in "have it on good authority"
3. a body or group to which an appeal may be made, such as a review board
4. a person or group who issues and/or enforces rules or laws, such as the legal and justice systems

I will define authority in the organizational sense, as **the vested legal right of a person to use organizational resources to attain organizational objectives.** Resources may consist of time, money, office space, equipment, subordinates, and so forth. Objectives may be to increase sales, increase return on investment, decrease labor turnover, raise productivity, and on and on.

Responsibility is another word with several meanings, among which are:

1. capability of responding
2. liable, in the judicial and/or control sense
3. maturity and conscientiousness, which applies to both persons and organizations

4. accountable, in the financial sense
5. adherence to the highest of desired values.

Defined in the organizational sense, **responsibility is the relationship existing between the person performing an assignment and the person who imposed that assignment.** If you will accept a definition of **management** as "getting things done with and through others," then you must accept the principle that a manager must delegate to subordinates in order for the objectives to be reached. Well, that's all well and good, but what is it that the manager delegates, **authority** or **responsibility?**

Certainly, if you expect someone else to carry out an assignment, that person must have access to the tools and resources in order to function. The delegatee will use them; you will not, as you have granted your subordinate this vested right. Accordingly, we could say that authority as we have defined it is what's delegated. But isn't there also some requirement on the part of the person assigned the task to act responsibly? Logic tells us yes, of course, so perhaps we should conclude that the subordinate is delegated both authority and responsibility. But not so fast! We've all heard that it is the head of an organization who is ultimately responsible for the organization's performance, and if this is true, the top manager can't delegate this responsibility. Perhaps, then, a subordinate is delegated only authority and not responsibility. Somehow that doesn't seem right either, does it? What about the other alternative? Could a subordinate be delegated the responsibility but not the authority to achieve the goal? No, that's ridiculous. That situation creates a fiasco.

Let's take these seemingly complex concepts and boil them down to their core meanings. I'll do that by stating **Fisher's Law #15.**

An act of delegation conveys and creates both authority and responsibility with respect to the subordinate. This conveyance/creation continues at each successive level of delegation. As a result, authority may descend in the organization to its point of need, effectiveness, and implementation. Responsibility, however, is accumulated, compounded, and fortified at each level in order of organizational ascension, so that final and ultimate responsibility culminates at the highest organizational level. As authority descends, responsibility ascends.

Always remember, you can't delegate responsibility away from you if you are the one in charge.

9

UNDERSTANDING AUTHORITY

Authority is a much-used and much-abused word, and not many people understand it as a basis for power and a force for action. You need to fully understand it in order to use it properly.

There are six types of authority, none of them necessarily mutually exclusive. That is to say, they can all exist in combination with one another. I'll take you through them.

1. **Coercion authority** is the use of physical force or the threat thereof to compel obedience and/or repress activity. At the height of a disagreement, you may have heard a superior say to a subordinate, or vice versa, "Let's go outside and settle this once and for all," as though pure physical dominance would transfer to the organizational relationship. It also happens that an organizational superior can exert a Svengalian mind control over a subordinate to the degree that the subordinate is a mental slave to the master superordinate. The forcing of one's will on another to do something illegal or contrary to company policy, for example, is a case of mental coercion. This is the rawest form of authority and should rarely, if ever, be used in an organizational context.

2. **Resource authority** involves the allocation and interplay of organizational resources from a superordinate to a subordinate. Budget allocations, information flow, office space assignments, bonuses, promotions, and numerous other examples of resources exist that can be meted out, or withheld, reflect the use of resource authority. I've always found it somewhat amusing how nice some

people are to others in the organization, irrespective of title or position, if they believe there is a current or potential resource allocation benefit that could involve them.

3. **Legal authority** is the most rational and common base found in organizations. It provides a vested right by law, organizational bylaw, charter, or policy, to engage in an activity. Most organizations and professions need a certificate or license from a governmental agency that empowers them to operate. At the individual level the appointment or promotion of a person is the organizational legality that gives the designee the right to function and use resources pertinent to the position. Press releases announcing promotions or appointments are more than motivational and recognition courtesies. They alert the world that the designee is now the person with whom to relate if one's needs encompass the designee's office.

4. **Identification authority** is the charisma or magnetism of the individual that gives that individual influence over others. When someone has "it," others admire it and are inspired by it, which causes subordinates or a constituency to do what the charismatic individual wants done. Politicians, as one example, often rely heavily on identification authority for their base of power.

5. **Expertise authority** is simply the combination of knowledge and experience applied to a given situation. If you know what you are doing and others don't, then you possess expertise authority over them, as you are the possessor of the relevant knowledge and experience. When a vehicle breaks down, for example, the mechanic who can fix it has the expertise authority, regardless of the lofty positions or titles of the passengers.

6. **Cultural authority** varies, depending on the culture and the environment. It's an authority born of deference to a group or individual, based on the customs and mores of that society. Some societies venerate the elderly, some venerate females, while others venerate males or the eldest male or female heir. Authority attaches to members of the group the culture deems worthy of authority influence.

Well, where does all this lead us, with respect to the lessons we can draw from this discussion?

Let me sum it up with **Fisher's Law #16.**

Of the six types of authority, coercion is the most repugnant; resource authority the most susceptible to manipulation; legal authority the strongest and most civilized; identification authority the most fleeting; expertise authority the most changeable, and cultural authority the most frail. Yet they all play a part in the authority base from which you do or will operate.

Always remember, authority must be used to serve those who grant it.

10

CONFRONTING CONFLICT CONFIDENTLY

It probably won't come as a surprise to you, but all organizations experience conflict. The trick is to make conflict constructive, not destructive.

Possibly you thought conflict, by its very nature, is destructive and detrimental to an organization, and therefore, you may think it could be ruinous in the long term.

It's true that many organizations let it get out of hand, and it results in a lot of wasted energy and turmoil, but let me tell you a little about conflict so you can confront it with confidence.

All organizational conflicts can be attributed to one or a combination of these four elements:

Organizational goals
Organizational means
Organizational resources
Personalities

Let's examine them one by one.

1. **Organizational goals** are subject to interpretation and therefore value assessments are attached to them by employees. Many organizations spend days, or even weeks, attempting to clearly and concisely articulate their vision statement, their mission statement, and their goals and objectives. Even then, words

will mean different things to different people. What does it mean, for example, to be "the leading organization in the field"? Will you target a select market, or a mass market? Do you want to be known as an organizational innovator, or do you equate stability with conservatism? Are you referring to financial values, press acclaim, or consumer surveys? You see the point. Reasonable people can have reasonable disagreements over organizational goals. So, overall, that example is not a very well-expressed vision statement.

2. **Organizational means** are also subject to employee interpretation and value infusion, and, accordingly, hold the potential for conflict. Let's assume for a moment that an organization wants to raise its return on shareholders' equity from 20 to 25 percent. How is this to be done? Should they triple the advertising budget; double the sales force; enter a new market; increase their debt; buy back some of their own stock; sell assets and lease them back; expand research and development; strike new relationships with franchisees, distributors, or suppliers; or all of the above? And if you do increase advertising, as one example, where do you place it–television, radio, direct mail, billboards, Internet–and in what proportion? Again, the point is obvious. There is room for reasonable and legitimate disagreement.

3. **Organizational resources** are always limited and scarce, as demand always exceeds supply. When you prepare budget presentations, you'll find this out in short order. Most employees will tell you they could do their jobs better if they had more help, either operating subordinates or staff assistance. This is an easy trap to fall into and leads to empire building. Don't succumb to it or you'll experience overhead overload, and that militates against a lean, streamlined, high-productivity organization. Still, competition for scarce resources is omnipresent and represents a source of conflict.

4. **Individual personality** conflict often arises out of the first three elements but usually occurs when employees emotionalize them. Personality conflict can often be instinctive, prejudicial, nurtured by stereotyping, or be based on a neurosis or psychosis of one or more of the employees involved. No matter what the root

cause is, personality conflict is the most insidious and injurious to the organization, and eruptions cannot be tolerated or condoned.

Let me state **Fisher's Law #17.**

Don't be intimidated by conflict! Manage it to a creative conclusion, encouraging rational interaction with a vibrant spirit, devoid of invective. Watch out for hidden agendas. Open personality conflict has no place in the organization; if personality pyrotechnics can't be corrected, eliminate the cause(s). The positive organizational environment has no room for petulance, egomania, deviousness, or duplicity.

THE BENEFITS
OF CONFLICT

Now that you know that you can never allow yourself to be intimidated by conflict, I need to tell you about the benefits of conflict, and there are benefits, surprising as it may seem.

Perhaps that sounds like an oxymoron, as possibly you never thought in terms of beneficial conflict.

1. Conflict serves to maintain group identity and solidify it. People have a need for group adhesion, and that can be strengthened when the group takes on an identity of its own and is given a formal or informal designation. People need a group identity as well as an individual identity, and conflict can help confirm that need and secure it. Project teams, task forces, and special units or squads are all examples of this dynamic.

2. Conflict can serve as a reason for existence and a frustration release. Groups working to achieve something are not as effective when others are not competing with them, wanting to beat them, or wanting to deprive them of their goal. An "adversary," real or imagined, tangible or intangible, is often necessary to spur the group into action. Frustration releases can also be directed at an adversary rather than at other group members. Adversaries serve a definite purpose. They can be the focus of directed activity and an emotional release.

3. Conflict can reinforce dedication to one's purpose by confirming determination to succeed. If something is worth protecting or seeking, conflict increases the desirability of it and the resolve to acquire or secure it.

4. The closer the relationship between competing groups, the more intense the conflict, the greater the degree of involvement of the participants, and the stronger the desire for total domination and supremacy. As an example, the most bitter and acrimonious battles often are those that occur between former friends or partners or through long-established rivalries.

5. Conflict is a measure of the stability of the relationship between competing groups. It often becomes ritualistic and ceremonial, as in labor-management negotiations. Such a relationship is beneficial, as it's better than an environment where there is no coordination, cooperation, or accepted custom. Some conflict is generated as an expected role or face-saving device, as when, for example, an auditor or inspector must find something wrong or to recommend or else others will think the audit or inspection is not complete.

6. Open conflict can clear the air if discord and discontent have been seething below the surface. Once in the open, the resulting emotional catharsis can allow all parties to recognize it, deal with it, and move on. Sometimes former adversaries become fast friends and former rivals become strong partners.

7. Conflict tends to unify your adversary, and it's more efficient to engage the battle with one opponent than with several, as your own resources can be used more effectively. It's better to fight one major adversary than to fight a swarm of smaller adversaries.

8. The most effective deterrent to internecine conflict is your knowledge of the strengths and resources of your adversary, and indications of such may be able to be determined only by probing or by minor skirmishes. Sometimes rumors are purposely leaked, for example, to identify and observe the reaction of potential adversaries.

9. Conflict can bring allies to your aid to assist you in your struggle. Such alliances can prove beneficial in other areas as well as in the area of conflict by building on those relationships. Politics do, in fact, make for strange bedfellows.

Let me sum up these comments on conflict as **Fisher's Law #18.**

Certain advantages accrue to every conflict situation. Exploiting those advantages strengthens your position. Since conflict can be managed, it is imperative that you do manage it, otherwise you will become the victim, not the victor.

12

ORGANIZATION:
THE ABSTRACTION

Let's play a quick word-association game. I'll mention a word and you tell me the first image that comes to your mind as the result of hearing the word. Ready? Here's the word–organization!

Quickly! Think! Let the first image develop, don't suppress it, express it!

"Organization!"

Well, the obvious question that now arises is what was the image you brought to your mind as the result of the word "organization"? I'll submit that the chances are nine out of ten that you let an incorrect, inaccurate, or ill-defined image seep through. Why? Because chances are you are used to thinking in terms of the tangible, the concrete, and the specific, not the abstract.

You may have thought of a building, a physical structure of brick and mortar, wood, glass, offices, the outside of an imposing edifice. If so, you equate an organization with an institution.

You may have thought of a diagram, commonly called an organization chart, with boxes and lines in some sort of configurative circuitry.

You may have thought of a mass of people, either in a collective body or segregated by boundaries of some sort, such as walls, partitions, or latticework.

Or perhaps you thought of a particular entity, the place where you work, an office building, a school, hospital, or other location that has specific meaning for you.

It's a normal reaction to think of an organization in those terms, so don't be unnerved by what I'm going to say. In a real sense, an organization is at once all of those elements, and at the risk of adding to the confusion, I'll offer the following: An organization is a system of interrelationships between or among two or more persons engaged in the pursuit of a common established goal. An organization is intangible in reality. It depends on people; indeed, it is people, but it is people working in an explicitly or implicitly defined relationship with each other. What's my point? Just this:

If you are going to be a successful manager, you've got to think of an organization not as a tangible entity but as an intangible system of interactions, transactions, and professional relationships.

All organizations rely basically on two elements in order to succeed: **planning** and **execution.** You may read or hear what others have said are the elements of management. The Frenchman Fayol, for example, coined the acronym POSDCORB, which identified planning, organizing, staffing, directing, controlling, reviewing, and budgeting as the spectrum of management. Other management buffs have either elaborated on or abbreviated this list, but it still all comes down to planning and execution. These two activities give rise to four possibilities:

1. Good planning and good execution
2. Good planning and poor execution
3. Poor planning and good execution
4. Poor planning and poor execution

Number one is the exception to the rule, and number four, regrettably, is becoming increasingly common. That leaves two and three. Which is preferable? Well, here is **Fisher's Law #19.**

A poor plan well executed is always superior to a good plan poorly executed.

Why? It's simple. Planning is done by a few—execution is accomplished by many. If many people are working in proper execution sequence, it's more efficient to refine the planning or change the planners. A smoothly functioning organization can change direction far more easily than an uncoordinated organization. Baseball managers and football coaches get fired if the team doesn't win. The team doesn't get fired.

By the way, here's another axiom, which is **Fisher's Law #20.**

> **Most people think in concrete terms, as opposed to abstract terms, most of the time. Don't get stuck in concrete.**

13

ORGANIZATIONAL VALUES

As you gain experience, you will understand that organizations possess and evoke values just as people do. That should not surprise you, since an organization is a network of people, and organizational values are usually a reflection of the personal values of the founder or the chief executive. I have found it best to match oneself with an organization that shares the same values as the individual, as that usually results in good personal and organizational "chemistry." A mismatch of values between the organization and the individual usually does not serve either well in terms of sustaining a long-term relationship.

Let me give you some examples of organizational values to illustrate the point.

1. **Competition–Compassion.** Some organizations are known for their fierce, intense, hyperaggressive competitive instincts and techniques. They stop at virtually *nothing* to expand their share of the market, win the account, pirate personnel, play accounting games to hypo the market price of their shares, stop just short of misrepresentation in their advertising, deride competitors through comparative advertising, and so on. Yet in these same organizations, the instinct and emotionalism of compassion can also exist. For example, many organizations have developed policies concerning donations and contributions to public works projects, educational programs, and charities.

In this sense, these firms are outstanding corporate citizens.

What is often muddled, however, is the purpose for which the "gift-giving benefit program" is used. Is it an element of an overall marketing strategy, a public relations tool, a sales promotion technique, a publicity stunt, a "we can afford it this year" impulse, or an act of contrition? The only economic justification for such gift programs is that the long-term benefit of the program will be greater, directly or indirectly, than its short-term cost. The social benefit is that society is enriched by such largesse, which adds to the quality of life, which, in turn, benefits the organization.

2. **Equality–Equity.** In human resource administration, for example, standards and practices must be developed and maintained to ensure equal and objective application to, and treatment of, *all* employees. In evaluating performance, however, based on differences in abilities, interests, aptitudes, and overall contributions to organizational goals, persons on the same organizational level must be differentiated. The task is not to treat each employee equally, but to differentiate employees so that each can be treated equitably. It's absolutely necessary to be "fair" to each employee, but fairness is an intangible, and if a fair judgment is based on an intangible circumstance, the decision is fraught with the potential for misinterpretation. How many hours have you spent with distraught employees who misperceived or rejected outright your "fairness" in handling their situation? The point is that equality of opportunity is not synonymous with–nor does it mandate equality in–the distribution of rewards, since performance and effort are rarely identical.

3. **Conformity–Creativity.** There are decided benefits to standardizing the organizational behavior of employees. If you train well, for example, a constancy of image, impact, level, and quality of product and/or service is the result. But to what extent does such mental and behavioral control inhibit creativity, which also has its benefits, and if allowed to function unfettered could be tremendously beneficial to the organization? I recognize that you can counter this point by stating that you allow for creativity within the broad boundaries of conformity, through informal meetings with employees, suggestion systems, brainstorming sessions, retreats, and so on, along the conform-create dimension.

There is a difference, however, between conformity and puppetry, just as there is between creativity and fantasy. Achieving the right balance is a constant challenge.

4. **Centralization–Decentralization.** Certain economies of scale, internal efficiency, fingertip control, and purchasing power often accompany centralized authority. Unfortunately, in some instances, so do inconsistency, mistrust, delay, misunderstanding, lack of confidence by the field force in headquarters staff, and demoralization. The advantages and disadvantages with centralization are often reversed with the advent of decentralization. On rare occasions it's possible to have the best of both worlds. For example, in cash management you can centralize collections but decentralize disbursements. The basic question is whether there is a concentration of authority or a distribution of authority, and in what areas.

There are many other organizational value comparisons that I could mention, such as the balance between innovation of a new concept and imitation, that is, taking and altering someone else's concept. Another value determination is between adoption of a code of ethics, for example, and adaptation, such as a compromise of principle in the vein of "when in Rome, do as the Romans do."

There are no textbook answers to these issues. You have to look at different organizations and decide what the best "fit" is for you.

Well, where does this leave us with this discussion? Allow me to set forth **Fisher's Law #21.**

> **Most anyone can make decisions on the basis of facts. A limited number of people can make decisions on the basis of timely interpretation of facts. The most far-reaching and significant decisions, however, are made on the basis of values.**

14

ORGANIZATIONAL COMPETITION

We now need to discuss another organizational dynamic, the subject of intraorganizational competition.

I suspect you frequently have been in a competitive situation within the various organizations of which you have been a part.

It perhaps started when you first realized you were a member of a group. That group could have been a family organization, grade-school class, Little League team, or whatever, and now you are part of an economic organization.

A question arises: "Is competition between and among the group members of an organization good?"

Your first inclination may be to say that it *is*, for the very word "competition" stimulates a reactive emotion within you that gives rise to an inner drive to express and release your own competitive prowess.

The nation's economy is based on the free enterprise system, of which competition is the benchmark, and we have been conditioned to the suggestion that competition brings out the best in all of us.

But does it? And if it does bring out the best, does it also bring out the worst?

Consider a training situation. A group of trainees is assembled and the trainer explains, demonstrates, shows, aids, coaches, and evaluates the individuals in the group in the performance of the task.

The trainer then inserts a competitive technique. The first person to finish, considering speed and accuracy, will receive a reward. Or the last one through will receive a negative reinforcement such as extra work, extra practice, working overtime, or additional assignments. Sound familiar?

What does this competitive technique really do? It identifies the above-average, average, and below-average trainees. Fine! But it's just possible that the above-average trainee performed well by nature of his or her superior general competence, previous experience, or characteristics peculiar to the training environment, materials, and/or performance time.

If the trainee has been habitually superior in past activities, the training exercise is another demonstration of it. If that's the case, that trainee may lose interest, become overconfident, and/or be condescendingly egotistical. Ho hum!

If the below-average performer has been habitually poor in past activities due to awkwardness, slowness, or whatever, the trainer has set conditions where once again this trainee's inferiority is confirmed. The trainee, therefore, condemns herself or himself to a legacy of poor performance, and the possible self-debasement syndrome deepens.

"Don't keep him/her," you might say! Okay, but bring in the next training group, and if the same competitive technique is used, you'll be turning some people out of that group too. If the organization can afford that type of training, "turn-in turn-out" activity, fine, you'll keep only the superior performers, but for how long? And those you keep may shake out if the same interpersonal competitive techniques are used on the job—which means you'd better oil the revolving door.

Take a second case. Several managers are placed in competition with one another; only their track record, market, location, and facilities are different. Under such different conditions there is no way that such competition can be conducted equitably.

I know you can cite examples of great turnaround situations, but those are the long shots, and besides, all the variables that happened to blend properly are peculiar to that specific situation.

By now you may think I'm speaking against competition. No, I'm not. I'm speaking against the misuse of **intraorganizational** competition, which is not to be confused with **interorganizational** competition. What constitutes proper use and misuse?

My answer is **Fisher's Law #22.**

> Interpersonal competition within an organization should occur only when there is a close commonality of competence, experience, resources, environment, goals, and other variables that will influence the outcome. In all other cases, individual self-competition should be employed, matching an individual's present performance with his or her own past performance.

In this way, the challenge is to better oneself, and you don't match a lightweight against a heavyweight. No one really wins in that case.

15

ORGANIZATIONAL
RECREATION

Organizational life is more than just the time you consider to be your work hours. You become identified with your organization, and it's with you twenty-four hours a day. Let's talk about the appropriate role for a leader in an organizational recreational setting.

In most organizations, occasions arise in which employees have an opportunity to "let their hair down." Such situations invariably involve a company-sponsored social event celebrating a holiday period, or marked business peak, milestone, or anniversary. Most industrial psychologists, human resource experts, and business consultants advocate such festivities for the creation or maintenance of group spirit, pride, morale, and bonding for the overall well-being of the firm. That's all well and good, but let's move from this "macro" approach to the "micro" approach. Specifically, what is the leader's role in terms of what the leader should do and not do at company social outings? We'll take one example to illustrate the point, but you can generalize the concept.

You are at a company-sponsored picnic and can participate in a pickup softball game, can act as the bartender, sit in on a poker game, engage in informal conversation by mixing, or cook the steaks, franks, etc. You are not a good softball player or cardplayer but have played both in other settings in the past. What would or should you do, given these three assumptions:

1. Your organizational position is higher than that of any other person in attendance.

2. You attend the function, for not to without a *real* reason could be misunderstood as unpardonable aloofness.

3. You don't purposely come so late as to "escape" these activities.

The pros, cons, and evaluations follow . . .

A) **Play softball**–You could be considered as a "regular" person and real team participant both on and off duty. This is the only possible organizational benefit. A personal benefit would be the exercise. Potential disadvantages could be a subversive attempt to make you look foolish, forcing errors, overextending the physical aspect by sliding, tripping, collision, or causing minor injury that would dampen the game and could be evident when back in the office. Others might cater to you since you are not a good player, thereby offering special privileges in a competitive circumstance, which would magnify your inability as a player. My evaluation is *don't play a sport unless you're good at it.*

B) **Be the bartender**–The advantage is that this role places you in a control position, which is one aspect of your management responsibilities. Simultaneously, it's a disadvantage since liquor can be behavior changing, and a perception can be advanced that you stationed yourself there to make moral judgments or informal professional evaluations. Whatever your intentions, others would think you were watching and counting, which would nullify group enjoyment. If anyone did overindulge and become abusive or raucous, it would be embarrassing to you as the "controller." Further, if someone fell victim to overconsumption, a guilt feeling could extend to and damage the working relationship. My evaluation is *don't be the bartender.* The only exceptions are if the activity is held in your home or at the organizational location.

C) **Play poker**–The sole organizational advantage is to be perceived as a "regular" person, but this situation is fraught with danger. Your economic status may open you to charges of "buying a pot." Cards can also lead to a test of wills of the participants where emotionalism overruns objectivity and good sense. Great gains or losses on the part of one or more participants could have serious consequences on working relationships. Pot or raise limits don't restrict the psychological relationships, only the economic ones. Participants could also spot your inclination to take risks or avoid risks, which can carry over to your professional life. My evaluation is *do not play poker with subordinates.*

D) **Mix informally and converse**–The advantage is that this innocuous activity holds little potential for detrimental effects. It allows you to mingle with others in a nonorganizational environment. You don't run any risk of appearing foolish, athletically so, or becoming an unspoken object of derision. The main disadvantage is that other participants may be unduly inhibited, expecting you to do something in the social situation that would serve to assert and confirm your organizational authority. This activity allows you to "leave early" with minimum disruption. As a personal note, you'll need a high tolerance for small talk–don't get trapped by one subordinate who wants to "get something off his or her chest"–and be careful of forming your own clique with your closest associates. My evaluation is that you touch bases for a "hello" to everybody. No omissions.

E) **Be the cook**–This depends on the prior planning of the activity. This role may have already been assigned. If not, there are many advantages to your undertaking it. It places you in a "controller's" position, but you're dealing with a food substance rather than a behavior-changing substance. The party's focus at some time will shift to food, and since the organizational focus is on you in the organizational environment, it's reinforcing to have this type of focus on you in the social environment. Gluttony on a sometime basis is not as stigma attracting as inebriation on a sometime basis. Further, this type of activity is easily delegated after the "rush," and barring culinary disaster, you will be the recipient of appreciative compliments. Further, you fulfill the expectations of many others in this "take charge" function and the transfer of responsibility acceptance from an organization scene to a social scene is on an equal plane. The disadvantages are personal, being only slightly inconvenient, perhaps. My evaluation is that *if the need and opportunity are there, cook the food, unless you are a terrible cook.*

Allow me to summarize with **Fisher's Law #23.**

Ensure that the nonbusiness activities you engage in with organizational subordinates informally reinforce established formal organizational working relationships.

There *is* a carryover effect.

16

ORGANIZATIONAL PHYSICS

There are some parallels that can be drawn between the world of science and the world of management. Allow me to give you some examples.

I'll relate to you the scientific principle, then I'll give you my counterpart management principle.

1. Essentially, Newton's first law of gravity says that "what goes up must come down." Here's **Fisher's Law #24:**

One who goes up must stay up—or go out!

---

2. Another of Newton's laws basically states that "a body at rest tends to remain at rest. A body in motion tends to remain in motion." **Fisher's Law #25:**

If you want something done, give the assignment to a busy person.

---

3. Archimedes studied fluids and determined that "any body, either wholly or partially submerged in a fluid, is buoyed up by a force equal to the weight of the fluid displaced." **Fisher's Law #26:**

> **Any manager, either wholly or partly submerged in a fluid—or by a fluid—eventually is going to encounter a pulled plug!**

4. Newton's third law states fundamentally that "if one body, A, exerts a force on another body, B, then B must exert an equal and opposite force on A." **Fisher's Law #27:**

> **Leadership is not unidirectional. It is a process of directed activity that must be met in equal and complementary measure of acceptance of that direction by subordinates.**

5. The Englishman Hooke found that "the deformation of a solid body is proportional to the force acting on it." **Fisher's Law #28:**

> **The formation and development of an organization is directly proportional to the commitment given to it.**

6. Doppler studied sound and postulated that "sound will change pitch depending on the movement of the source or the listener." Think of a train whistle on a moving train, or a car horn on a moving car. **Fisher's Law #29:**

> **The greater the organizational communication distance, the less you will be heard and regarded.**

7. The Frenchman Le Chatelier propounded that "whenever action is taken to change an existing physical system, the system reacts in such a way to oppose such action." **Fisher's Law #30:**

> Whenever action is taken to change an existing organizational system, the system reacts in a way to delay that change and alter such change in a manner that most closely resembles the original system.

8. I'm not sure who it was who studied light and came up with this principle: "The angle of reflection equals the angle of incidence." **Fisher's Law #31:**

> Face issues squarely, not obliquely, and make decisions on the basis of facts and values, not emotion or personal relationships.

9. Einstein's theory of relativity states that "absolute true and mathematical time, of itself and from its own nature, flows equally without relation to anything external." **Fisher's Law #32:**

> Do it right the first time. You may not have a second chance.

Those parallels get to the heart of a lot of organizational dynamics; you can learn more from the different fields of science than just matters that are internal to the discipline.

17

V. I . S . I . O . N .

It is a frequent lament throughout much of the nation that leaders in all walks of life–politics, business, education, et al.–are lacking in the VISION that can serve as a driving force to achieve goals that take us beyond mediocrity. Critics suggest that we have lost sight of basic ideals and lofty aspirations that, if realized, could propel the country forward in elevating the quality of life for all Americans. VISION is also a cornerstone for economic organizations that need a focal point from which to articulate their concept of the reason for their existence, or as the French would say, their raison d'être. Encompassed within the statement of VISION is the organization's mission statement, the definition of terms (to prevent misinterpretation), and the guiding principles upon which the organization relies for the conduct of its activities.

Let's look within the word VISION itself for a better understanding of what it's all about.

1. **Values.** The core underpinning of VISION is the values the organization professes and stresses. Sometimes the values are projected by the founder(s) and carried on by successors, or sometimes they accrue to the organization as the result of its interaction with its environment. Such values may rest on the philosophical bases of quality, customization, service, immediate response, customer accommodation, employee support systems, community involvement, etc. Other philosophical bases may emphasize mass production and marketing, processing, procedural response, customer guidance, employee direction, community observation, etc. Values give meaning to goals and objectives and influence organi-

zational relationships and operations. The **V** in VISION also represents veracity, valor, and victory. An organization needs to be consistent and true to its values (veracity), which, if achieved, gives it lasting credibility. It also needs to act with courage from time to time (valor), taking the high road where an alternative may appear easier or more expeditious. Finally, the organization needs to perform and execute at ever-ascending levels of excellence in order for it to grow and thrive (victory).

2. **Insight.** The stewards of an organization, be they founders or successors, need to have this sixth sense that there is an opportunity that can be fulfilled, a hurdle that can be surmounted, a niche that can be established, or a challenge that can be met. It's the mental "lightbulb" that some people experience that displays the way to do something and the means to achieve it, that makes things fall into place. It's the unfolding path that is revealed that shows the way and stirs action and progress.

"I" can also stand for **i**nstinct, **i**ntuition, and **i**nspiration, for within each of these words lies the emotive power that causes excitement, movement, development, and accomplishment.

3. **Standards.** Organizations cannot realize a merit-worthy VISION without establishing standards in every realm of its endeavor. Without standards, chaos reigns, inconsistency and lapses abound, and a descending spiral of unacceptable performance envelops the organization. With standards, benchmarks are identified, measurement occurs, consistency is the standard operating procedure, an improvement culture is cultivated, excellence is recognized, and accelerating propulsion undergirds the organization's activities.

The S can also stand for **s**tability, **s**kill, **s**trength, **s**upport, and **s**ignificance. Standards lend themselves to each of these concepts, which has an uplifting effect on the entire organization.

4. **Innovation.** Trail-blazing, groundbreaking, pathfinding activities require innovative thought, creative approaches, a "think outside the box" mentality, and an unshackling of custom-bound, "business as usual," conventional, and traditional ways of doing

things. Leadership that allows, indeed encourages, the open expression of reflective ideas is crucial to the visionary process. This "I" can also stand for **i**nvestigation, **i**ntroduction, and **i**nstruction. Investigation is required to test the feasibility of the VISION, including the rearrangement or removal of environmental constraints when they appear. Introduction is the presentation of the VISION to the constituency who will participate in its formative stages, and instruction is the counsel given to the constituents as to how to proceed to realize the VISION.

5. **O**rganization. Moving from the the theoretical to the practical, the hypothetical to the workable, requires organization. All purposeful activity is based on some form of organization, the component parts of which function discretely within themselves but are also interlinked with one another so that there is a synchronization and mobilization of collective effort and proportional results.

The O can also stand for **o**rder, **o**bjectives, and **o**utcomes. The organizational framework gives order to values, insight, standards, and innovative thinking that are part of the VISION. Objectives are the established, measurable mileposts that are developed that represent "the reach" to which purposeful activity is directed. Outcomes are the measured results of the activity at established points of time.

6. **N**ormality. When a VISION has been conceived and the foregoing progression has evolved, the realization of that VISION becomes the new normality. The combustion of the VISION elements gives rise to great expectations, acceptance, appreciation, and an uplifting of the quality of life, product, or service that was the venue for the VISION. Economic history is replete with examples of VISION becoming reality, and that reality becoming commonplace, before yet a new VISION appears.

The N can also stand for **n**etworking, **n**ourishment, and **n**egotiation. The completion of a VISION results in its extension, usually by a network of some sort (franchising is one such example). Continued nourishment (refinements for the sake of improvement) and negotiation (licensing is one such example) are both a part of the normalization process. Without VISIONaries, the world would be a pretty dull place.

Fisher's Law #33:

It's not too late to develop *your* vision. It's also not too early.

18

TAKING THE LEAD

In order to be a successful executive, you need to understand fully the concept of leadership. Not many people really understand it; that's why there is constant attention being called to it. There is a lot that needs to be said, so let's get into it now.

There has never been a universally accepted definition or explanation of **leadership.** There have been several theories advanced as to who a leader is, what a leader is, and what a leader does.

Trait theory has attempted, unsuccessfully, to identify the single physical and/or personality trait, or blend of traits, that identifies a leader. Nothing has ever been concluded definitively or conclusively.

Role theory has focused, insufficiently, on the functions of the leader. That is, does the leader establish goals or implement means to reach goals, or, if both, in what proportion? Does the leader revise goals or intensify existing goals and/or means? Role theory has never really distinguished between an administrator, a manager, a policy maker, an executor, and a leader.

Intent theory analyzes the acts of leaders in terms of what their motivations are as manifested by their actions. Are they group oriented so they spend time establishing and strengthening the interpersonal relations of group members, that is, attending to group maintenance and group hygiene, or are they interested primarily in coaxing the group to accomplish its objectives, focusing on group achievement?

More recently, **plural leadership theory** has suggested that no one person can exert all the forces necessary to attain a desired result in a group context, and leadership is shared to some extent among some or all the members of the group. This, perhaps, tends to cloud the question rather than clarify it.

While it is complex, there are some things we can say with certainty about leadership:

1. Leadership resides in a person. Machines and signs can't lead; they can direct, but inanimate objects do not lead.
2. Leadership is easier to detect than it is to define. We can recognize it when we see it but have difficulty analyzing it and articulating it.
3. Leadership should not be confused with positionship. A position holder is not necessarily a leader. A position holder can be a tyrant, manipulator, resource controller, dictator, authoritarian, and yet that person won't be considered a leader.
4. A leader must have a following of one or more persons. Leaders lead people; a cattle herder, per se, is not a leader.
5. Leadership is fluid and changeable, depending on the person, the group, and the situation.
6. The group must accept the efforts of the leader freely for leadership to occur.
7. The situation must require a leadership act for leadership to occur. Leaders have to *do* something. Leadership is active, not passive.

Here is my definition of leadership. **It serves as Fisher's Law #34.**

> **Leadership is the art of seeking attainment of organizational goals through working with, over, and/or under other persons, by securing their willing cooperative efforts while simultaneously satisfying individual and group personal and professional developmental needs.**

Oh, I know you can find fault with this, but before you do, consider:

1. Leadership is an art, not a science. It emanates from within the person rather than existing in objective reality.

2. A leader seeks attainment and keeps seeking it. Even when goals are reached, new goals are set and the effective leader continues striving on behalf of the group.

3. The leader works with, over, and/or under other persons. A leader does not always have the top position, yet as a subordinate, a person can be the unmistaken leader of the group. The leader can work with others as a first among equals or over others. Leadership and positionship do not always coincide.

4. "Willing cooperative efforts" involve the follower's free will and efforts with no coercive element existing.

5. Satisfy **individual personal** and **professional** needs–personal needs are physiological, safety and security, belonging, esteem, self-actualization, to know and understand, and aesthetic requirements as categorized by Abraham Maslow. Professional needs are to communicate, to strive to accomplish, and to gain recognition, among others.

6. Satisfy **group personal** and **professional** needs. Groups have the same personal needs as individuals but on a collective basis. They also have professional needs such as group identification, a productive environment in which to function, and a sense of achievement.

A leader must be able to pull from the front, push from the rear, and nudge from the side. Imperfections will occur; you must accept that but not tolerate it. Leaders make sure that any mistakes that are made are made only once.

Realize that leaders make the uncommon common, the difficult easy, the unthinkable thinkable, and the inactionable actionable. They also motivate, delegate, empower, and inspire followers.

19

LEADERSHIP TRAITS

It is true that no single combination of traits has ever been identified that guarantees a person will be a leader with every type of group, in every kind of situation. Life, and leadership, are not that simple.

There is, however, some evidence of leadership traits that have proven successful.

Some traits have been identified through extensive research that are characteristic of leaders, but it's not foolproof and the absence of one, or the presence of another, is not any guarantee. Nonetheless, it is instructive to know what those traits are so you can nurture them. Here they are:

1. **Intelligence**–successful leaders possess and are perceived by group members to possess an elevated degree of intelligence relative to the average intelligence of the group. Group perceptions often confuse "possession of knowledge" with innate intelligence, however. Further, excessively superior intelligence on the part of a "leader" can result in ostracism, subterfuge, or bemusement by the group. It can work against you, but generally, demonstrated intelligence is an absolute requirement for organizational success.

2. **Desire for excellence**–successful people evidence a constant pursuit of perfection, a striving to reach beyond the ordinary to a level of astonishing achievement. This trait often manifests itself through a wide grasp of, and attention to, detail. Frequently, this detail consciousness is perceived as "pickiness" by less perceptive subordinates unless the broader foundations of personal

and professional competence have been laid firmly by the leader, and are demonstrated and reinforced on a continuing basis.

3. **Conscientiousness**–is the conscious acceptance of the responsibility of the position, an understanding of one's role in the organization, and the thoughtful use of authority. One should not be trapped by the "I wouldn't ask you to do anything I wouldn't do myself" syndrome. One person has only so much mental and physical range. It varies. The conscientious executive will *delegate* in good faith, and won't *relegate* simply out of mental/physical necessity. Leaders are perceived to put in more hours willingly, and more into the hours, than the average group member, which is the tangible and visible evidence of the executive's acceptance, understanding, and commitment to the role and to the organization.

4. **Diligence**–fierce tenacity to the accomplishment of objectives, both short term and long term, is a characteristic of the successful executive. The "stick-to-itiveness" exhibited by the leader's organizational attention span precludes wanton dissipation of resources by "riding off in all directions at once." Leaders also recognize weak spots and losses prior to the average group member and are not timid in altering resources or reshaping objectives in light of those circumstances.

5. **High upward mobility drive**–has been identified to exist at the personal level, versus the organizational context, in successful leaders. They seek to be known as persons of impact, influence, and presence. They view this as a means of accumulating increased amounts of responsibility channeled to defined or created organizational goals. They **accept praise and adulation but are not affected by it** except as a reinforcer of the mobility drive.

6. **Self-confidence**–leaders have tremendous faith in their own abilities and in their own judgment. They look to their own developed standards as a basis for their actions and are not swayed by bandwagon psychology or the "go-along-to-get-along" precept. They are independent of, but not removed from, others. They rely on good eye contact and exhibit honesty, integrity, and the "habit

of command." They are not befuddled or immobilized by new situations; rather, they handle them directly and adeptly.

7. **Extroversion**–group members perceive successful executives as mixing and mingling among them freely with no self-consciousness. Leaders are active persons, finding reward and enjoyment in personal interaction, and contribute measurably to the facilitation of both professional and social communication interchange. Successful executives who have "risen from the ranks" exude an air that sets them apart from–not necessarily above–the group of which they were once a member or are now leading.

8. **Communication capability**–involves two elements. First, the successful leader is one who can view and summarize group thinking and sentiments quickly and accurately. Second, the leader is an individual who possesses more information than the average group member. Often this is a function of the communication flow coming into the position, from which the incumbent benefits, who then is the communications receiver, coordinator, filter, synthesizer, and distributor. A person holding such a position is at an advantage compared to those who have only a piece of the total picture. One who can distill a mélange of facts and feelings and summarize them in a cogent, articulate manner without demeaning their complexity is in command of the situation.

9. **Humor**–leaders have been measured and found to possess a constructive sense of humor. They have the ability to laugh at themselves and do not feel threatened by the injection of humor that is in proper perspective, occasion, and tone in the organizational context. They are not intense to the point of no return, retaining the ability to step back from the situation and assess it with a fresh pair of eyes, which sparkle with a trace of excitement and levity.

10. **Team player**–the group's perception of a leader is culturally based to some extent. The strong leader is expected to represent, through personification, action, and vocalization, the values and goals of the group. To this degree, the leader is the group's "good example" and is the projection to all outside the group of the

symbol and substance for which it stands. The leader is one of the group, but is a "first among equals." The leader is rarely perceived as manipulative of people, only of inanimate resources, and maintains constant attention and reference of the group's goals.

11. **Planning**–leaders spend considerable time planning. Successful executives plan for both the short range and long range, continually relating aspects of the one to the other. The leader must be simultaneously shortsighted and farsighted, possess foresight as well as hindsight, insight as well as oversight, a molar view as well as a molecular view. Planning gives purpose to the organization. Leaders know, and are perceived to know, where they are taking the organization.

12. **Decisiveness**–leaders are decisive in the actions they take. They are not encumbered by self-doubt and do not reflect on regrets in hindsight. They know the hardest decisions of all are "people decisions." It does not mean they act quickly, act on inadequate information, or are rigid once committed to a course of action if subsequent events change. It does mean they set the direction, and then move toward it, making "course corrections" as necessary.

This list is not exhaustive, merely representative of what a lot of research has determined to be traits possessed by leaders generally conceded to be successful executives.

Let me summarize these thoughts as **Fisher's Law #35.**

> The successful executive has established an emotional balance between organizational accomplishment and personal growth, has a sense of unfulfillment with regard to what remains to be accomplished, and possesses the resources and authority to effect greater accomplishment.

20

LEADERSHIP QUALITIES

Since we have discussed leadership traits, we should now move to examining leadership qualities. Allow me to set the stage and then we'll address some essential qualities necessary for success.

Success in the executive managerial ranks rests on the elements of the leader, the group, and the situation in interaction with one another. The group and the situation are often fluid—emerging, converging, diverging, resurging—in a cyclical and, hopefully, progressive pattern. The leader must recognize these stages of group and situation dynamics and bring skill, talent, and capabilities to bear on them. This is not to say the leader must be a chameleon, changing colors as it were, depending on one's mood. It does mean that a leader must call from his or her innermost personal resources that element or combination of elements in just the right proportion, and with just the right degree of intensity, to draw the utmost from the group as it interfaces with the situation to achieve organizational goals.

Earlier we identified some key traits that successful leaders possess. We now go beyond the identification to determine what belief and behavior patterns successful leaders exhibit in their relations with others.

Truly successful leaders are generous people, not necessarily in the financial sense but in recognizing that their talents, while residing in their person, in fact belong to the organizations they serve. Their contributions and satisfactions take force not in their giving or receiving but in the activating, for they know that it is through activity that expression and creativity give rise to organizational and personal development. In that sense, they know it is nice to give and receive, but it is better to activate.

The successful leader believes that success comes from competition, not largesse or monopoly, and that competition does not, in the total sense, involve the destruction of competitors, but their fortification and resolve, which in turn is stimulative and developmental to the organization. There is no shrinking from competition or challenges; rather, there is a hard-nosed resolve to conquer it.

The successful leader knows that success is the mastery of a situation but that success is accompanied, however slight, by a fear of failure based on a possible change in the situation, or a change in society's values as to what was once desirable turning to undesirability. Since we cannot conquer unpredictability, we are forced to live with it. The leader does so, however, with rationality, poise, professionalism, a secure confidence, an aura of courage, and a buoyancy of spirit.

Successful leaders have a mature appreciation of the complexity of the decisions they make relative to the uncomplicated minds they may have possessed earlier in their careers, when matters were "simpler" and the "right" decisions seemed so much more obvious. Yet they do not require a crutch to escape complexity; rather, they find enjoyment and solace in the analysis of the very factors that go into the decision-making process.

Leaders condense their organizational leadership roles into a relatively few fundamental operating notions. They are persons of recognized intellectual capability, and although detail conscious, they are not detail confined. They match their overview with their purview and, consequently, are objects of esteem and respect by their subordinates.

The successful leader possesses a guarded trust of others, having experienced both the joy of subordinates working to and beyond their capability and the disappointment due to the tragedy and treachery of human failings. The organization is viewed neither as a corporate jungle nor a corporate infirmary, but as an economic and social system of which the leader is a part and for which the leader has full responsibility.

Successful leaders are adept at seeing an interconnectedness to

events that the average person sees as isolated, unrelated inci-
dents. Consequently, they have a mental framework for decision-
making purposes that simultaneously is expansive and precise.
Their ability to see and draw relationships among these things that
impact on their organizations provides them with the "sixth
sense" on which they can take action. They think both strategically and tactically.

Let me conclude with **Fisher's Law #36.**

**The successful leader demands and receives a sharp per-
formance edge from the organization, which gives it a
competitive edge, frequently becoming a cutting edge,
resulting in a winning edge.**

It's good to be on edge.

21

LEADERSHIP STYLE: THE IMPERIAL EMPEROR/EMPRESS

Let's get practical at this point and talk about leadership styles. There are a lot of styles that have a lot of names, but I've witnessed three fundamental approaches to the practice of leadership. We'll discuss each of them, but I'll start with the "imperial emperor" or "imperial empress." I'll exaggerate a little, perhaps, to emphasize the points, but a lot of people really are imperial in large part, whether they admit to it or not. Let's take a peek at their mind-set.

1. **Employees are lazy; they don't want to lead, they must be led.** "You employees fall into the same category as cattle. You're meek, mild, timid, lack direction and intelligence, and would follow anyone who promised you comfort, convenience, and security. You don't know the meaning of leadership, and if you did, you wouldn't want it. You are indolent, stupid, devious, and self-indulgent. That's why control systems and security systems are necessary. As good fortune for you, I am here to provide you with leadership and direction. I'll take care of it; it's my management burden. I'll organize and direct things; just do as I say. I'll even help you organize and straighten out your personal life, since you're most likely incapable of that, too. That's why we have a credit union, or I make personal loans to you and call my contacts when you get into trouble."

2. **Might is right.** "I'm more powerful than you are and don't you ever forget it. Don't ever cross me. I've got more money than you do, I'm smarter than you are, and I could crush you if I wanted to. I have more and better political, economic, and social contacts than you can ever hope to have, and if you do cross me, I'll see to it you never get a job in this city, this state, or this industry as long as you live. You're an adult, and you know on which side of your bread your butter is spread. You're on a limb and I've got the saw. Now that we understand one another, just do as I say. Don't talk, I don't want to hear it. Just do it and shut up. Discussion closed!"

3. **Win at any cost.** "Most of you misguided souls have heard and believe that human values, principles, and standards exist in organizations. I've never heard of such garbage in all my life. You'd better believe that the only things in life that have value, principle, and standards are the budget and the bottom line. Survival of the fittest applies to organizations, as does the law of the jungle. It's the big green that counts, and, if I have to stomp on others to get it, I will. Nothing personal, but I'll stomp so hard, I won't be pestered again. I may have to lie, cheat, swindle, stab others in the back, break my word, bribe, evade taxes, shade things, and slander. My regret will be if others do it to me before I do it to them. Don't be shocked; this is not peculiar to me. Look at other organizations and you'll see the same thing."

4. **Fear is my motivator.** "When I walk in, I want you to stand up, bow your head, and lower your eyes. When I say jump, you'd better ask 'how high?' I don't want to hear anything negative, and if I even get a hint that you are resisting what I tell you, we'll color you gone. I'm ultimately the one who hired you and I'm the one who can fire you. After all, there are certain and definite advantages to dismissing people from time to time. If you don't believe me, try me. What's that? You want to try me?"

5. **Act precipitously; keep employees in a state of confusion.** "I go away for a few days and when I come back, this place looks like a nuclear meltdown. What did you do, all take vacations, or did you just party all the time? I guess the old bromide proves true—when the cat's away, the mice will play. Well, the top cat is

back and I'm docking your pay, and some of you won't be here next week. Don't expect any time off from now on. I try to be fair and you take advantage of me. We're going to have to review our human resources policies, I can see that. Why do I have to be surrounded by such incompetency?"

6. **Retain all credit for positive events.** "We've had a good year this year–thanks to my leadership, the many hours I've put in, and the foresight I've displayed. Our organization has grown, obviously as the result of my acumen and performance. Someone once said that no one is indispensable. Don't believe it, I am. I had my picture in all the media representing you. Never mind what the reports said–is it my fault commoners don't recognize genius when I'm with them? We achieved some record highs this year, personnel turnover, complaints, and threatening phone calls. That was your fault. I don't know what this world is coming to!"

7. **Escape adversity!** "Of course, there are some things that haven't gone very well this year, but it wasn't *my* fault. If you employees had just done what I told you, everything would have been all right. Why do I always have to come into the middle of things and do it for you? The IRS says there are some irregularities in our books, but I always said you could never trust accountants. They said I directed them to make some questionable entries, but no one has it in writing. Besides, I have a memo that I wrote to the file on the matter at the time of our conversation and the memo says the opposite of what is alleged. By the way, I've just put Percy here in charge of operations, and he told me he was going to trim the workforce by twenty-five percent. Didn't you, Percy? Speak up, Percy."

8. **Glamorize tokenism.** "But all in all we came out pretty well this year. Yes, it was tough, but I did it. As an expression of my appreciation to you, I want you to know that I'm raising your salaries one dollar per week. That annualizes out to fifty-two dollars per year. We'll also take the locks off the rest room doors for an additional five minutes in both the morning and the afternoon for your convenience. I've called a press conference to announce these groundbreaking measures to the media."

9. **Create chaos to reinforce power and authority.** "We're going to be making some changes around here. I'm not at liberty to say what they are, but you'll find out soon. Then we'll see what you're made of. Also, that vacation schedule I approved for everyone last week, I had to throw it out. I'll make the vacation assignments. That way you won't have to worry about submitting a request. And in fifteen minutes we're going to shut down for thirty days for some interior renovation."

Of course, the imperial emperor or empress is not as blatant as I've portrayed here. They are much more subtle and clever in dealing with others. Yet their behavior, and what is said from time to time, as well as how it is said, gives clues to their management style. Let me express **Fisher's Law #37.**

The imperial style is effective when the group is comprised of nonvoluntary participants with little or loose interrelationships between and among group members and when the group is heterogeneous in character and is comprised of persons who are conditioned, used to, and comfortable in a power relationship. It is also effective when the situation is one of emergency or crisis. Under *any* other conditions, in terms of management style, the Imperial Emperor/Empress needs a new set of clothes.

22

LEADERSHIP STYLE:
ANGELS

We have seen that the imperialistic leadership style, except in unusual circumstances, is a repressive, power-based approach to managing people. Now we need to discuss another style of leadership that, in my experience, most young people try to adopt—until they become scarred by experience. I call it the angelic approach.

Let me describe organizational Angels to you, exaggerating a bit, once again, to illustrate the point.

1. **Employees can be self-directed.** "I'm very fortunate you employees decided to work here, and I'm thankful you decided to come in today. As I let you know by word and action, your maximum development can be achieved by free expression and unsupervised activity. Any supervision on my part would be restrictive and harassing and, even if I did give you an idea or suggestion, that would be dictatorial and controlling. I have complete faith that you see what needs to be done, and because you seek activity as a natural part of existence, you'll *do* what needs to be done. I believe that the one who supervises least supervises best, so I'll stay out of your way. The situation will guide most of your activity; I won't have to."

2. **Right is might.** "I fully subscribe to the 'I'd rather be right than be president' approach to management, because righteousness always prevails. We may have some temporary setbacks from time to time because some misguided people will take advantage

of our honesty, generosity, and faith in them, but they'll learn the error of their ways. It'll all come out in the wash sooner or later. Things have a way of balancing out. We know we're right in what we do, and that's the only source of strength on which we need to draw. We can remain above the adversarial and confrontational aspects of life. If the IRS says we owe, then we pay. If customers complain about anything, we always give them double their money back or don't charge them."

3. **Rules were made to be broken.** "Some organizations have rules and regulations, but we don't need to be encumbered by these things–that's for others. I've never seen a rule yet that wasn't broken, so why have rules if you're going to make exceptions? The exceptions just lead to more rules. Regulations are an imposition on one's freedom, and we don't want to have that atmosphere here. We really don't need standards either, since they are artificial. All of us are different anyway, and we can set our own pace. I've heard others say that policies were 'guidelines.' That's a wishy-washy, mealy-mouthed approach to things, and the answers to a lot of tough questions are passed off as 'policy.' That's not going to be the case here."

4. **Organization is a family.** "We're just one big happy family in this organization, and I look after each and every one of you with immense personal as well as professional interest. That's why I've not said anything to you when you came in late or didn't show up. You don't need me to add to your troubles. I regard you as my family, and I know you look at me in the same light. That's why things are always upbeat and positive in this organization."

5. **Free communication–up, down, and sideways.** "We as management have nothing to keep from employees, and that's why I always copy everyone in the organization with all letters and memos. Yes, it adds to paper cost and the administrative distribution system, but no one can say you're not informed. I believe in open communication. I even keep all of you informed when we're contemplating major organizational changes–that's participative management. My door is always open. Any of you can see me at any time about anything. I know I'm always in a meeting when

you attempt to come in, but that's participative management too. I just don't know where the time goes."

6. **Gives all credit to others.** "We've had a good year this year, and it's all thanks to you. I didn't really have anything to do with it. I just fill a figurehead role here; you ladies and gentlemen are the ones to be congratulated. You're the ones who make things happen here. I'm the luckiest person around to have you working here. You're so good, you leave me with nothing to do. That's the sign of a good manager."

7. **Refuses to recognize organizational problems.** "We don't have any problems here. Every once in a while a challenge arises, but no problems exist. Like the time an employee was discovered taking a personal computer out the door on the last day of work. The poor guy just wanted to improve his skills, and that's commendable. It's true we've had some customer complaints about the service they've received, but then again, you can't please everybody. The accountant insists on using those red figures on the operating statement, but you have to admit it makes for a colorful report. Things will work out, don't worry about it. Time will take care of everything, and we'll get it behind us."

8. **Foolishly generous.** "I believe in taking care of our people and their personal needs. Gloria broke her one-inch fingernail typing this morning, and I told her she could take the week off until it grows back again. Our salaries are the highest in the industry; golly gee, wish I could say the same thing about our productivity. I'm more than fair minded, I'm fair handed. If you're having trouble doing your job, I'll be glad to jump in and do it for you. It's good to get back to basics, anyway, with a hands-on approach."

I suspect that you've known Angels in organizations at one time or another, usually for a short time, though, since they don't survive. But why? They're well intentioned, have a good attitude, and have a pleasant personality, generally speaking. I'll tell you why! They deal emotionally, not rationally. They look for and often see the depth of matters but not the breadth of matters, thereby blinding their mental perspective and mobility. They have never reconciled the concepts of political and spiritual equality with differences in individual capacities, motivation, and values. They rely on flight rather than fight. They are more sensitive than sensible, prone to self-doubt rather than self-confidence. They often panic easily or are passive to a fault. They unwittingly sacrifice leadership for companionship, recognition for resignation, report for rapport, effect for affect, conclusion for occlusion. They are functioning idealists rather than functioning pragmatists. They absorb problems rather than deal with them. They seek popularity, confusing it with respect. They confuse professional responsibility with a blurred concept of human relations. They can do irreparable harm to an organization, destroying any semblance of planning, organization, authority, or control.

In short, always remember **Fisher's Law #38.**

Don't be a managerial Angel!

23

LEADERSHIP STYLE:
THE PRAGMATIST

I will now describe the third basic leadership style found in organizations, what I call "the pragmatist."

"Is this leadership style better than the other two?" you may ask.

Better is a relative term, but let me describe a pragmatic leader's style to you and we can then identify the relative merits.

1. **Perceptive analysis and judgment of people.** The pragmatist recognizes that a continuum exists over which to measure the desire of people to seek purposive activity. The pragmatist is not polarized in the viewing of subordinates as competent–incompetent, lazy, active, sincere, insincere, etc. Pragmatists, rather, are unusually adept at evaluating subordinates, recognizing the gradations that exist on a multidimensional measurement scale. Their judgment of people is not infallible, but they can size up others quickly, being accurate far more often than not. They do not rely on first impressions, and their "sixth sense" and "inner eye" can cut to the core of others with whom they relate. They supplement their beliefs in the original three elements for business success–LOCATION, LOCATION, LOCATION–with an equal portion of a second set of three additional important elements for success–PEOPLE, PEOPLE, PEOPLE–and a third set of elements–TIMING, TIMING, TIMING.

2. **Right is might, but it needs an offense and defense.** There is perceived and actual integrity, honesty, character, and objectiv-

ity in the pragmatist's relationships with others. This aura, which is set for the entire organization, is both contagious and pervasive. The pragmatist recognizes that some issues have equally valid "right" but opposing solutions, but pursues what is best for the organization, and is on the "right" side of the question if not "right on" the question, in the view of others. The pragmatist's personal and organizational rectitude and righteousness are impenetrable, and the pragmatist does not get drawn into conspiratorial webs with politicians or competitors. The pragmatist knows that the best offense is an immovable defense, and the best defense is an unstoppable offense, to use a football metaphor.

3. **Plays by the rules.** Unlike the Emperor, the pragmatist will not go to extremes to win. Unlike the Angel, pragmatists know specified objectives, and a path to reach them has to be set for the organization to operate effectively and efficiently. There is a personal and professional code of behavior by which they operate and will not violate. They do not lie, cheat, swindle, scandal, libel, bias, evade, bribe, conspire, pander, or vindictively inflict damage on others. They live by the philosophy that they do better to, and more for, others than they expect others to do to them, knowing that in this way, they can't lose.

4. **Respect is rooted in attainment.** The pragmatist does not want to be feared, knowing that a fear-hate-insecure organizational environment is counterproductive to organizational and personal development. They do not seek "love" or popularity because they don't need it, having egos that are developed well beyond that stage. Their moments of satisfaction and fulfillment are predicated on the organization working as smoothly, professionally, and perfectly as is humanly possible. They seek respect for their organization, and its success is what they cherish most in their professional lives.

5. **Communicates effectively.** Pragmatists do not give all information to all subordinates, thereby smothering them in paperwork, overwhelming them with verbiage, and taking up their time in a welter of meetings. Neither do they shroud themselves in secrecy or mislead others for the purpose of staging a personal

power demonstration. Pragmatists provide information, and a system for information flow that allows others the knowledge and coordination they require or desire to function expertly in their own capacity. Pragmatists write well, speak articulately, and possess expressive features and gestures.

6. **Shares credit for accomplishment.** Pragmatists are the first to recognize that credit for organizational achievement is due and attributable to everyone in the organization. Their very attachment to the organization has some influence on the results attained. If not, then the organization is overstaffed. While pragmatists distribute and acknowledge credit commensurate with the contributions of others, they also evaluate continually the performance of subordinates in the light of changing goals, methods, and the external environment. Pragmatists are also not afraid to make hard decisions when hard decisions are called for.

7. **Accepts the mantle of the office.** Pragmatists do not delegate the responsibility and authority for confronting the less desirable aspects of their role. Nor do they ignore problems and let them fester. They do not shirk responsibilities for honest evaluation, communication of nonoptimal results, assessment of subpar employee performance, high-level discussion with dissatisfied customers, stockholders, etc. They do more than seek to solve problems. They seek to prevent problems.

Let me summarize the pragmatist's style with **Fisher's Law #39.**

A. The pragmatist knows that in every respect, substance is far more important than appearance.

B. The pragmatist knows that professionalism is contagious and is therefore the consummate professional.

Well, it should be obvious, you may think, that the pragmatist's leadership style is certainly better than the other two, but let's not jump to conclusions too quickly. We have yet to talk about groups and situations, and the leader is only one part of that dynamic context. I can understand why you think as you do at this point. Before we move on, let me give you some erudite advice that I call **Fisher's Law #40.**

You need to read people and situations as accurately and as quickly as you read books.

24

KNOWLEDGEABLE
LEADERS

I want to conclude the several points we've made on the subject of leadership with what leaders themselves know about the subject. This is the knowledge leaders have gathered through observation, experience, and their own insight.

1. Leaders know that success comes in cans! It doesn't come in "can'ts" or "cannots." Leaders know things should be done, *can* be done, and they do them.
2. Leaders know that the measure of a team is not how well the team performs when things are going as planned, but how well the team performs when things are not going as planned.
3. Leaders know that it is their attitude, not their aptitude, that determines their altitude in life.
4. Leaders know that the most important investment they will ever make is in their integrity.
5. Leaders know that the most important asset they will ever own is their reputation.
6. Leaders know that the most important expenditure they will ever make is the time they give in service to others.
7. Leaders know that the most important thing they put on when they get up in the morning is their smile.
8. Leaders know that when they are faced with a choice between intelligence and experience, they will choose experience. With intelligence you often get arrogance; with experience you usually get wisdom.

9. Leaders live their life through a zoom lens, not through a rearview mirror.
10. Leaders open their mind before they open their mouth.
11. Leaders know that small minds talk about people. Great minds talk about ideas.
12. Leaders realize that when they become comfortable they become vulnerable.
13. Leaders possess a lot of **WIT**. **Whatever It Takes.**
14. Leaders know that "winning" starts with "beginning."
15. Leaders know that self-confidence comes from internal mastery. Effectiveness comes from external mastery.
16. Leaders don't let bad experiences make them bitter. They know it makes them better.
17. Leaders know that life is not to be measured in terms of an "unbeaten season." They know that there will be times when they may lose, but they'll never allow themselves to be defeated.
18. Leaders know that sustained leadership rests on the four cornerstones of ethics, courage, standards, and performance.
19. Leaders know that "vision" not only involves eyesight, but also involves insight and foresight.
20. Irrespective of title, leaders know that they are CEO's: Competent! Effective! **Organized!**
21. Leaders don't tolerate mediocrity, for they know mediocrity is a step toward degeneration.
22. Leaders know that their improvement attitude is a daily endeavor.
23. Leaders realize that success is not an individual achievement. Many people participated in it: subordinates, customers, teachers, mentors, and coaches, among others.
24. Leaders know there is a difference between positionship and leadership. The former rests on power, the latter rests on consent.
25. Leaders impact situations in greater measure than they allow situations to impact on them.

Now, all of these leadership underpinnings could each be their own Fisher's Law. But let me summarize it all with **Fisher's Law #41.**

Leaders know leadership rests on a platform of loyalty, excellence, attitude, determination, energy, responsibility, standards, honor, inspiration, performance. In a single word, it's called leadership.

25

GROUPS

Now we need to turn our attention to the subject of groups, be they employees, volunteer associations, social gatherings, or other types of assemblies.

A leader, by definition, must have a following, and in the realm of human relationships, followership usually involves groups of people. We need to look at who they are, what they are, what characteristics they possess, and how they should be measured, from an organization's viewpoint. It is a simultaneously complex but intriguing subject.

Let's get definitions out of the way, recognizing that definitions can vary according to purpose but realizing the necessity to start from a firm, accepted foundation. A **group** is a collection of two or more persons assembled as the result of a perceived need or desire to affiliate with one another to satisfy that need or desire through a personal interrelationship. The needs and desires may or may not be the same for each participant, and the intensity of the need and desire may differ. There does not necessarily need to be continuous visual, written, or audible communication, although it's a rare group that doesn't communicate regularly. The perceived expectation of affiliation of a participant with other group members and the bonding that arises therefrom can give rise to group behavior, and is what separates a group from a set of individuals, a mob, a crowd, or an audience. A **formal group** is an assembly of persons activated for an express purpose known to the participants. Examples are business organizations, school classes, and so on. An **informal group** is a meeting of persons for an unspecified purpose more for the benefit of the participant as an individual than for achievement of a designated goal. Examples are a kaffeeklatsch, or a pickup lunch-hour bridge or chess game. Informal groups often evolve into formal groups, and formal groups sometimes deteriorate, in function, if not in title, to informal groups.

Another analysis that can be made involves the voluntary or involuntary nature of the group. A **voluntary group** is one that can be entered and left freely. Examples are associations and political parties. An **involuntary group** is one on which there is a limitation as to the ease of entry and departure. The military is an example. Groups can be elected, such as a board of directors; selected, such as corporate committees; occupationally required by a license, such as lawyers and CPA's; honorary, such as medal of honor winners; exclusive, such as insurance or real estate million-dollar round tables; or secretive, such as a "fifth column." As you see, groups can be categorized over several criteria.

Okay. You're now the leader. You've got a group to lead. Have you ever really considered the profile of the group you are leading? Why not? The effectiveness of what you want done will be determined in part through its acceptance by the group. Don't relate to your people only on an individual-by-individual basis without considering group dynamics. Here are some characteristics of groups of which you should be conscious in order to have an optimal relationship.

1. **Size**–Is it a small group or a large group? Small groups usually foster frequent and close communication. Seven or fewer persons usually define a small group, while more than seven is usually considered a large group.

2. **Stratification**–Who is assembled? Is it a subgroup of a larger group? Is it everyone in the organization? Department heads? One department? Unit managers? The day shift? Remember that status differences between and among group members can lead to status affirmation ploys by higher-status group members and inhibition on the part of lower-status group members.

3. **Homogeneity/heterogeneity**–What is the degree of similar socially relevant and demographic characteristics of group

members, such as socioeconomic status, age, interests, gender, and work experience? Homogeneous groups usually coalesce faster than heterogeneous groups, for better *or* for worse.

4. **Familiarity**–To what degree is there a mutual acquaintance-ship of group members to one another's personal lives and relationships outside the organization? High group familiarity can lead to a stronger tie to group loyalty than to leader loyalty.

5. **Efficacy**–To what degree is the group operating efficiently as a unit? Groups that work well together could resent any personnel changes in the group. They can freeze new employees out, for example.

6. **Compatibility**–To what degree is mutual respect, agreeableness, and visible cooperation evident among group members, versus contentiousness, one-upmanship, conflict, and contempt? Open conflict can be dealt with by the leader more easily than group-protected internal hostility.

7. **Commitment**–What degree of significance does the group hold for its members–intense loyalty, benign neutrality, marginal to hostile participation? Strong group identity can lead to immense achievement by the group, and vice versa.

8. **Accessibility**–With what degree of ease can one be included in the group? Is it open to everyone? Is it an "inner circle"? Restricted? By invitation? Does it represent an accomplished feat to have "arrived" as a group member? The higher the standards for group participation, the greater the probability for group achievement.

9. **Control**–To what degree does the group regulate the behavior of its members? What are group expectations and chastisements for absence, tardiness, inappropriate remarks, or attempts at dominance by one member of a subgroup? A leader is often well advised to let the group administer its own control mechanisms rather than exert his or her own authority.

10. **Flexibility**–To what degree are the group's activities marked by informal behavior rather than rigid adherence to specific procedures? Casual directed behavior can often lead to greater sustained group accomplishment than specified behavior.

11. **Autonomy**–To what degree does the group act independently of other groups? Does it take assignments from other groups or does it determine its own activities? An autonomous group will usually achieve at a higher level than a dependent group.
12. **Participation**–What is the level of time and effort participants devote to the group's activity? Does it extend beyond the assigned tasks and time so that group members volunteer extra effort and time to ensure completion of the group's objective?

Let me sum up our discussion of groups **as Fisher's Law #42.**

Any group, the participants of which are in frequent contact with one another, will develop a group personality that is *different from, and more than a composite of,* the personalities of its members. The group personality will be both a reflection of and a reaction to the leader. A designated or an appointed leader entering the group's environment must learn to deal with the group personality as well as the personalities of individual members.

I know this may appear to be somewhat academic, but it's important to understand the dynamics that can come into play. Just think back how many times you've been surprised at the outcome of a meeting in which you have been a participant. Group factors were at work!

Think about the groups of which you are already a part. You'll see how easy it is to examine them. Analyzing groups is only the first step, however. We now have to look at how the characteristics we define affect group behavior.

26

GROUP BEHAVIOR

We have just concluded that groups have a personality of their own over and above the combination of personalities of the group members. Now we'll discuss some aspects of group behavior about which a leader should knowledgeable, in order to get the maximum performance out of the group.

1. **When first assembled, groups are poised with expectant attention.** The dynamics of the first meeting, or the first meeting after a period of time, are crucial to the subsequent performance of the group. The spirit of the group members is generally high, their minds are fresh, and physical fatigue has not set in. Group members are curious about and eager to receive or form their own direction. Many a meeting has been "lost" at its inception due to faulty performance in the opening moments. First impressions are semipermanent impressions in a group setting. Above all else, lead with your strength when first approaching a group.

2. **In a group setting, the notion of "impossibility" is reduced.** Part of the group personality syndrome is to mentally or vocally demean the difficulty or impossibility of an assigned or suggested task. Often this is the result of the bravado of one or more key group members, but just as often it is the reluctance of the group, or any member, to acknowledge a "can't do" attitude. As group members jockey for recognition and status within the group consciously or subconsciously, a feeling of "I/We can do anything–let's get going" often pervades the group. Just as individuals can exceed apparent human limits on occasion, groups can too. Consequently, group involvement can hypo individual effort, which in turn can

result in the group's superior performance. Athletic coaches call it momentum. The trick is to maintain *perpetual* momentum.

3. **Groups foster a sense of diminished personal responsibility.** It is axiomatic to say that the larger the group, the greater any individual member's anonymity. As a result, the general responsibility for group actions is distributed over the members and shared by them in an equal or predetermined proportioned manner. Thus, a single group member other than the leader does not have sole responsibility, which can affect the group's judgment. This is why every so often a group will go off "half-cocked," whereas if each of the members had been approached individually, the results might not have been the same. The leader is ultimately responsible, of course, but when the group is making decisions, the leader is simply the representative or spokesperson of the group, even though the leader may be perceived to provide direction and channel activity. The elected leader functions primarily as the group's shining example. The selected or designated leader is the focal point of decisions, and most group members will not feel a compelling personal responsibility for them.

4. **Unless specifically assigned reporting responsibility, most group members will not premeditate carefully and in total perspective the purpose or desired outcome of the meeting.** Group members, usually due to the press of time engaged in their own functioning, will not devote much time to preparation for the group meeting they are about to attend. An exception occurs when a group member has a particular point or program he or she wishes to present and have accepted, but even then the member's attention will be devoted to that aspect rather than the total overview of the group's functioning. The group perceives the leadership to hold responsibility for coordinating, integrating, and summarizing group direction and activities and is correct in this anticipation. Consequently, group members will press for what is important to them, realizing other group members and their desires will be a moderating influence. The fundamental principle in bargaining strategy is to ask for more than you expect to get and are willing to accept. Group members know this, and it is one reason individuals in the group usually accept leader judg-

ments that temporize their initial position. When a group member cannot accept the outcome, the member usually severs affiliation with the group.

5. **A group setting is conducive to exaggeration.** Exaggeration of benefits accruing to the group, threats to its existence or performance, and praise or criticism of the group will occur informally and travel rapidly in a group environment. This is due in part to what the group and its participants hear, versus what is being said. There is a tendency to amplify the good news or bad news from member to member in cross discussions as each group member wants to be sure every other group member reacts with the same degree of understanding and intensity. Usually the loudest, not necessarily the most rational, voice dominates. You can attain a "fever pitch" faster in a group setting than you can in dealing with individuals on a one-to-one basis.

6. **A group setting is conducive to polarized thinking.** Ideas, suggestions, or opinions presented to groups are usually accepted or rejected in totality rather than analyzed for positive and negative elements. A large group is an excellent base for criticism but is less so for creative implementation, except for brainstorming sessions. Most group members will recognize extreme positions or ideas; some group members will differentiate and place themselves in between the two "poles," making it difficult to find the exact solution acceptable to these members. Consequently, many decisions coming from a group represent the "least detrimental" rather than the "most far-reaching" position.

7. **Contagion is rapidly and easily accomplished in a group setting.** Groups are given to impulsive behavior more so than the average individual. There is a greater impetus to transform suggestions into action and demand immediate achievement. This is due in part to the stimulation each participant enjoys as the result of being a group member and the tendency toward emotionalism that stems from being in an interpersonal setting. Frequently, this desire for action manifests itself in the demand for appointment of subcommittees, since most group members recognize the limitations of large groups.

8. **A group will structure itself with respect to the roles participants play in meetings.** As group members become familiar with one another through communication interchange, they will establish their own niche in group activity. For example, one participant will frequently remind others of the basic objectives of the group in analyzing the current discussion or activity in order to maintain focus on those objectives; most every group has, and needs, a person who provides comic relief; someone will act informally as parliamentarian if a formal designation has not been made, and many participants will settle into their own roles. Once developed, it's difficult for individual members to change their role. If they attempt to change, initial efforts will be met with some degree of chastisement by other group members, as change represents a disrupting impact on existing group dynamics.

9. **Groups rely heavily on symbols.** Recognizing that people are more transitory than institutions, and desiring an allegiance to an impersonal representation of the group rather than blind loyalty to a leader, symbolism plays a major role in congealing the group. The use of symbols can transcend differences among individuals within the group and act as a unifying element for the total group. Symbols represent visually the "higher purpose" for which the group exists and can go a long way in preventing fractionalizing of the group. An organization's logo, flag, and statues are examples of such need-fulfilling symbols.

I'll summarize this discussion of group behavior with **Fisher's Law #43.**

Group effectiveness usually falls between the maximum possible and the minimum allowable. The result rests with the leadership, which must use group dynamics to achieve what is best achieved in a group setting. Sometimes it's better not to assemble a group. Other times it's better to advise individuals as to what you want accomplished prior to group assembly.

27

SITUATIONS

Now that we have discussed several aspects of leaders and groups, we must turn our attention to an equally elusive element of the leadership syndrome–the situation. At the outset, we must state the obvious. Whereas leadership characteristics are bound by the personality, depth, and range of talent and flexibility of the person occupying the leadership position, and the group character tends to change only as the leadership changes or individual members enter and leave the setting, situations are highly volatile, fluid, and fleeting. In fact, the "situation" is never static but is perpetually changing since it encompasses both the external and internal environments. Still, situations can be analyzed and categorized, and it behooves the leader to approach *all* "situations" as being manageable.

One must first consider factors over which the organization has virtually little or no control. Such factors include an abrupt change in the world or national economy, the issuance of a new governmental regulation, resource scarcity such as a utility cut down, the appearance of a competitor in the same market area, natural disasters, and so on. There are some external factors, however, over which the organization can exert some control. These include community involvement activities; having employees run for local office; and sponsorship of local, regional, or national events that invite good public exposure. This is known as being "proactive."

Internally, events can also occur over which the organization has little or no control. Examples are heavy employee absence due to illness or destruction of company assets due to a calamity such as a flood or fire. Finally, the internal environment can change because of factors that are generated internally. Examples would be decisions to enter new market areas, expand the product or service line, change human resource policies, or acquire or divest divisions or subsidiaries. Given these four aspects of organizational existence, we can set up a matrix of possibilities as follows:

Environment

EXTERNAL	INTERNAL
Stable	Stable
Stable	Unstable
Unstable	Stable
Unstable	Unstable

1. **Stable-stable environment**–represents the most desired state, and is what most people mean when they say it's "business as usual." External and internal elements are predictable, and a slight change on one side of the environment is balanced quickly and accurately by adaptation on the other side. Changes that do occur are planned or forecast, and there are no big waves in the organizational waters. A state of flux always exists, of course; that's why we have daily reports. Generally speaking, however, the systems employed by an organization are working, and an atmosphere of relative calm and normalcy prevails. The leader enjoys the finest luxury–time. Harsh authoritarian and autocratic methods will meet with spoken or unspoken employee rejection. A solicitous or nonexcitable approach by management is expected and may even be appreciated.

2. **Stable-unstable environment**–is the next-easiest situation to manage since the focus can be on the internal instability with only normal attention being given externally, until the in-house situation is remedied. Depending on the nature of the internal instability, management can activate the contingency plan. Yes, that's right, you need contingency plans. Many matters of internal instability reside in the personnel area and can be overcome by promotion, transfer, reorganization, overtime, temporary hiring, use of consultants, or change of personnel policies. In such circumstances, the leader must, and is expected to, act quickly and

decisively. You've got to preplan. Authoritative action carried out quickly and efficiently gives rise to the group's perception of your "habit of command" and can reinforce the charisma of the leader.

3. **Unstable-stable environment**–represents a frustrating management problem in that instability in the external environment is largely perceived as being beyond the influence and control of the leader-manager. The singular benefit is that the internal organizational environment is relatively stable, allowing for primary focus on the outside. It is in this situation that many leaders mentally if not physically capitulate to circumstances and operate under the "I can't do anything about it" syndrome. The true leader rises to the occasion and guides the organizational ship through the stormy waters of unpredictability. This involves complete and efficient communication flow from subordinates as well as outside sources so that assessment of the situation can be kept current. Decision making in an unpredictable environment is hazardous at best and catastrophic at worst. Sometimes the best decision under such conditions is to do nothing different until the situation clears up. The world cannot stand incessant unpredictability, and consequently the external environment will "settle down" after a relatively short time, although some irreversible changes may have taken place. The leader may need to "buy time" as best one can, for precipitous decisions can be as disastrous as procrastination. On the other hand, one cannot be immobilized, and consistent recognition of that point in time when it is necessary to act or not to act is what separates astute leaders from all the others.

4. **Unstable-unstable environment**–represents the worst-case situation and often stems from the cause-and-effect relationship of the external environment on the organization. Bankruptcies and dissolutions do occur. This situation calls for leadership heroics and one whale of a lot of luck, but good leaders have a hand in making their own luck. Strong authoritarianism is essential, expected, and perceived as resilience. Management attention must be fairly equally divided between the inside and outside environment, as changes in one area will necessitate a balancing action in the other. The greatest financial and human toll is exacted in such circumstances, but so are the greatest satisfactions. The external

environment is likely to settle first. This situation often results in the mental and often physical resignation of management. It is under such circumstances that your world sees what you're made of. The ultimate measure of management is at hand.

Well, let's sum up this discussion of the situation with **Fisher's Law #44.**

The effective leader impacts the situation in far greater measure than the situation impacts the leader.

28

BUREAUCRACY

As you know, organizations are hierarchical structures, and work flows within such structures generally follow an input-throughput-output pattern. There is a concept that identifies this process, and it's called "bureaucracy." Now that we have discussed the dynamics of leadership, groups, and the situation, we need to turn our attention to an understanding of bureaucracy so you will be able to manage it to a productive end. Definitions first, so we have a basis for developing our insight.

A bureaucracy can be defined as "an organized system of bureaus, divisions, or departments, each overviewing a prescribed functional area and scope of activity for which it has authority to act, coordination of which occurs through a stepped series of higher-level responsibility and authority centers, the culmination of which is vested in the highest office." That's a mouthful, I know, but that's the way it is.

Bureaucracy has one striking feature. It exists in every realm of organized human activity. Before I proceed, it's necessary to state **Fisher's Law #45,** as subsequent discussion is based on it.

> **Bureaucracy is essential to the efficient and effective functioning of institutions. Its efficacy needs to be measured in terms of its concept as well as in terms of its conduct.**

Those words are self-evident if you stop to think about them. Bureaucracy is the natural outgrowth of the specialization of labor, which itself evolved as the result of the industrial and agrarian revolutions and the development of society. The advent of the concept of labor specialization was as significant to management science as the discovery of fire and the wheel were to civilization. As labor specialization proliferated, the need for unity of direction and coordination of effort became obvious. The tiered organization we now speak of as a bureaucracy evolved as it met those needs. Bureaucracy has its advantages and disadvantages, like everything else. Here are some of its advantages:

1. Bureaucracy allows for a division of labor that generates a high level of *individual* expertise.

2. Authority but not responsibility can be delegated, and resources can be allocated to the different offices or bureaus.

3. Bureaucracy provides for review or appeal procedures, and lower-level activity and decisions can be scrutinized by higher levels of authority. Ideas can be refined. Errors can be remedied.

4. Policies can be developed to address frequently arising issues.

5. Standards can be established to apply uniformity throughout the organization.

6. Economies of scale can benefit those the organization serves.

7. Monumental objectives can be reached through a directed, concerted unity of effort. A collectivity of linked individuals is stronger, and is capable of an enlarged scope of activity relative to a series of isolated, unconnected individuals.

8. Responsibility and specific authority can be pinpointed and documented, and performance can be measured individually and collectively.

Here are some of the disadvantages, of which you must also be cognizant:

1. Labor specialization can reduce acceptance of personal responsibility by employees for the total end product or service.

2. Employee perceptions of the stated objectives can be widely diverse.

3. Policy application and the meeting of regulations can become ends in themselves rather than the means to the end of serving those the organization purports to serve.

4. Communication and coordination is susceptible to distortion in multitiered vertical structures.

5. Personal service can give way to impersonal "red tape" processing.

6. Bureaucrats sell their services to the organization in return for a paycheck and may have no stake or pride in ownership, which can result in labor turnover. This can be assuaged in the private sector, however, by stock options, profit sharing, and pension plans.

7. The decision-making process is often slow and cumbersome.

8. "Staff" specialists may not really understand "line," or operational, problems on which they are asked to assist, and operations personnel may not understand staff specialties and language.

The design of bureaucracy is not nearly as important as the ability of the leader to measure its performance against predetermined objectives. Here is **Fisher's Law #46.**

> **The smaller the organization, the greater the personal duty placed on the leader. The larger the organization, the greater the management responsibility placed on the leader.**

Perhaps you have always regarded the word "bureaucracy" as pejorative. But it does have its good points, too. Interesting!

29

LEADERS VS. BUREAUCRATS

Now that we have talked about leadership, groups, situations, and bureaucracies, I feel compelled to point out some differences between leaders and bureaucrats. It's all in the mind-set and the approach to life and work.

Here are some differences between leaders and bureaucrats:

1. Leaders say "We can do it." Bureaucrats say "It'll never work!"
2. Leaders look for continued progress. Bureaucrats are overly proud of the status quo.
3. Leaders exhibit and inspire an improvement attitude. Bureaucrats are self-satisfied.
4. Leaders look for opportunities. Bureaucrats wait for something to happen.
5. Leaders "play a good game." Bureaucrats "talk a good game."
6. Leaders judge themselves. Bureaucrats hope others will judge them favorably.
7. Leaders know they must confront problems. Bureaucrats hope problems will go away.
8. Leaders demand flawless administration. Bureaucrats get bogged down in administrivia.
9. Leaders delegate duties and tasks. Bureaucrats absorb duties and tasks.
10. Leaders are comfortable with their subordinates. Bureaucrats are comfortable in their offices.

11. A leader says "I'm responsible." A bureaucrat says "It's not my fault."
12. Leaders can laugh at themselves. Bureaucrats are offended by bureaucracy-directed humor.
13. A leader shares credit. A bureaucrat claims the credit.
14. A leader says "I'll take the blame." The bureaucrat says "Who's to blame?"
15. The leader is a tireless worker. The bureaucrat is a tired worker.
16. When things get hot, the leader is overwhelming. When things get hot, the bureaucrat is overwhelmed.
17. The leader goes for "the win." The bureaucrat goes for "the tie."
18. The leader rises above adversity. The bureaucrat runs away from adversity.
19. The leader is outgoing. The bureaucrat likes going out.
20. The leader is often the team's "most valuable player." The bureaucrat is often the team's "most voluble player."
21. Leaders develop subordinates. Bureaucrats assign subordinates.
22. Leaders say "We can fix that." Bureaucrats say "I told you it wouldn't work."
23. Leaders are customer oriented. Bureaucrats are process oriented.
24. Leaders provide direction. Bureaucrats give instructions.
25. Leaders can manage many things at once. Bureaucrats prefer to manage one thing at a time.
26. Leaders handle the media effectively. Bureaucrats allow the media to handle them.
27. Leaders earn respect. Bureaucrats demand respect.
28. Leaders seek organizational commitment and loyalty. Bureaucrats require personal commitment and loyalty.
29. Leaders trust key subordinates. Bureaucrats rely on control systems.
30. Leaders plan for the future. Bureaucrats let the future unfold.
31. Leaders recruit the best talent available. Bureaucrats don't want to be challenged by subordinates.
32. Leaders teach. Bureaucrats pontificate.
33. Leaders emphasize standards. Bureaucrats emphasize discipline.

34. Leaders focus. Bureaucrats watch.
35. Leaders inspire. Bureaucrats perspire.
36. Leaders manage the stress in their lives. Bureaucrats are managed by the stress in their lives.
37. Leaders communicate articulately. Bureaucrats communicate artfully.
38. Leaders lead for the future. Bureaucrats manage for the moment.
39. Leaders take action at the appropriate time. Bureaucrats react only when necessary.
40. Leaders say "We succeeded in spite of the obstacles." Bureaucrats say "We could have succeeded if it hadn't been for the obstacles."
41. Leaders take advantage of the rules. Bureaucrats go strictly by the rules.
42. Leaders see the glass as half full. Bureaucrats don't see the glass.
43. Leaders are generous with their time. Bureaucrats are protective of their time.
44. When things look as if they are going wrong, leaders cry "charge!" When things look as if they are going wrong, bureaucrats cry "foul!"
45. Leaders are gracious. Bureaucrats are ingratiating.
46. Leaders are aggressive. Bureaucrats are intrusive.
47. Leaders think strategically. Bureaucrats think about time off.
48. Leaders attempt to be objective. Bureaucrats can be swayed and influenced.
49. Leaders are selflessly motivated. Bureaucrats are selfishly motivated.
50. Leaders enjoy their time. Bureaucrats put in their time.

One of the very best pieces of advice I can ever give you can be found in **Fisher's Law #47.**

Don't ever allow your organization to be run by bureaucrats.

30

EXECUTIVE CHARACTER

There are a number of definitions of the word "character," but the meaning of the word we're talking about in this Fisher's Law is that essential quality and pattern of behavior found in an executive who underpins his or her moral constitution, from which emerges the executive's personality and reputation. If character is the core of an individual, then it becomes important to identify the elements of character possessed by successful executives so others can adopt or develop them as part of an executive growth process. The following are seven elements of executive character, the presence and mix of which can cause one to be an effective and successful executive.

1. **Authority** is a bi-modal quality. *Personal* authority refers to demeanor, presence, body carriage, a manner of speaking, personal charisma, a way of interacting with others, react-ability, and a self-controlled, self-paced command aura born of self-confidence and past experience. *Professional or organizational* authority is the vestiture of an individual to use and allocate resources commensurate with the position he or she holds. This is conferred authority as opposed to emergent authority and can come about as the result of a position offer, promotion, election, selection, or appointment. In this circumstance one is cloaked with the "authority" of the office held. The effective executive needs both types of authority. One without the other is not nearly as good as having sufficient quantities of both.

2. **Decisiveness** is the character element that recognizes the acceptance of the responsibility for making decisions in a timely

fashion, in an objective manner, and after weighing all the available facts and evidence. It does not refer to a rashness of action, rigid inflexibility, or necessarily a quickness of pronouncement. It embraces focused determination and clarity of goals with a resolve to reach those goals. It also embraces a sense of movement in that decisiveness is part of a dynamic process that causes timely action to occur. It is the forerunner of action.

3. **Inspiration** is another intangible character element that causes others to lift their efforts well beyond their normal level because they are imbued both intellectually and emotionally with the rightness of their activity due to the example you set and/or the communication ability you have exhibited to them and that serves to fuel their extraordinary effort. A number of executives can inspire others for a short period of time and/or can inspire others when they are physically present with them. An effective leader can inspire others over a sustained period of time and without being physically present all the time. That's why political and business leaders are prone to have their pictures adorn as many visible areas as possible, since they can't be personally present everywhere at all times. They hope that their image will be enough to constantly stoke the fire in the belly of their followers.

4. **Integrity** is the character element that embraces fundamental, instinctive honesty, a worthiness of self, a reliance on one's words, and predictable behavior that a person will always take the high ground morally and ethically in relationships with others. Integrity can come both naturally (innate behavior) or be gained environmentally (learned behavior). Integrity is not piety, nor is it sanctimony. It is inwardly cemented and outwardly manifested as opposed to being inwardly manipulated and outwardly controlled. Integrity is absolute, not relative. Anything less than total integrity constitutes some measure of dishonesty.

5. **Empathy** is the character element that causes you to be able to place yourself in the other person's mind and shoes so you can see things from that person's perspective and feel things from that person's emotional context. Equally important, it also encompasses the ability to exude to others that you understand their

_ sition and perspective (even though you may not agree with it). Empathy is the second step in any successful negotiating process. (The first step is recognition that there are divergent positions or perspectives.) Empathy does not necessarily connote passion, sympathy, sentimentality, or acquiescence. It is simply the ability to go "out of mind and body" (yours) and into the other person's (or group's).

6. **Receptivity** is the character element that displays openness to people, ideas, and possible changes in the way of doing things and to new or different experiences. Receptivity involves an attitude of being approachable, of listening intently, of not letting preconceived notions block communication, and of respecting the dignity of others in their relationship to you. Receptivity is not passivity, nor is it automatic acceptance. It does embrace both sensitivity and sensibility coupled with a desire to grow (both personally and organizationally) through alertness to new opportunities and/or refinements to existing opportunities. It is the opposite of imperviousness. It is a smile, eye contact, courteous speech, appropriate body contact, etc.

7. **Vigor** is the character element that conveys spirit, movement, activity, and an unyielding quest for progress that is evident to all who surround you. It encapsules forward motion, resiliency, upbeatness, drive, and determination. It does not convey hyperactivity for the sake of activity, a "make work" philosophy, an "all talk and no action" orientation, or a "no talk and all action" form of behavior. Vigor is both mental and physical. It's steady, not fluctuating; active, not passive; perpetual, not sporadic. It is the essence of life led to its fullest.

Fisher's Law #48.

Build executive character; don't inhibit it or destroy it.

31

THE DOOR

Let's talk about some management issues and techniques that you will likely face and will have to deal with in the course of your career.

I have known a number of managers who, because they read it or heard it somewhere and thought it sounded nice, professed to have an "open door" policy in their organization as part of the relationship they attempted to foster with their employees. In one specific case, I was told by one of my managers, "I have an open door policy in this organization. My people can get to me at any time about anything!"

On the face of it, this exclamation seems virtuous, democratic, pleasant to say, and pleasant to hear. The only trouble is that this "policy" *doesn't work,* and I have never known anyone who professed it to really live by it. In fact, I have known managers who became the object of derision by employees as the result of their management hypocrisy based on the divergence of stated philosophy with actual performance.

Let's analyze this "policy" in light of its intent, content, and desirability. Clearly, it behooves you to create an environment whereby all your employees feel they can, and in fact *can* see you concerning matters for which they have not gained satisfaction and for which you could assist. The additional psychological advantage is obvious, of course, in that the employee's perception of self-importance and organizational concern are heightened since you have made your time available. If an employee visits you in your office, the physical trappings are often enough to cause the employee to minimize the problem and to absorb every word you utter as though it's gospel. No matter what the outcome, the fact that you listened and perhaps extolled is organizationally supportive and reinforcing in and of itself. Those are the advantages.

On the other hand, if you allowed this procedure to operate unchecked and without control, you could get little else accomplished and you'd have to replace your carpet or tile all too frequently. Still, to have an open door policy and then keep the door closed is self-defeating. You may counter by saying that many problems can be solved directly at lower operating levels or with staff assistance and should not be brought to your attention in the first place. True enough. Unfortunately, however, many employees will not accept a decision as final until it reaches the pinnacle of the organization.

It's not really a dilemma if you remember **Fisher's Law #49.**

Do not have an open door policy; rather, have an "accessible door" policy. Make it clear that you are not available at any time for anything but can be made available if absolutely necessary only after all other possible remedies and resources have been applied. You are no more "interruptible" than is the employee in the course of his or her normal job.

While I'm thinking about it, permit me to make another point about employee relations. It's **Fisher's Law #50.**

Every manager should meet personally every new employee assigned to the manager's physical location on the date of hire, or as close thereto as possible. Area, district, or regional managers should personally meet new employees at each location hired since the date of the last visit.

It's a wise investment in human capital.

32

CONTROLLING CONTROLS

The word *control* has a variety of meanings, yet most people think of it, initially anyway, in its negative sense. In organizations, control is usually equated with a restraint or restriction on what one is allowed to do. The regulatory sense of the word has a bad connotation, as in the phrase "they control everyone who works for them." We take that to mean that there was a manipulative or disproportionate influence or restraint to the working relationship that would place the subordinate in the role of a mechanical instrument or a puppet. Most of the meanings of "control" are, in fact, not negative. For example, in scientific research, a control group, as opposed to an experimental group, is the basis of measurement against which the results of the experiment can be determined. The controls of a vehicle govern its direction, speed, turning capability, and so on. In the management sense, "control" means a system of orderliness and organizational discipline and functioning in combination with internal and external security measures. It is not repressive or restrictive; rather, it is illuminating, as it assigns responsibility and, therefore, highlights proper functioning as well as malfunctioning. We will now discuss controls with a three-part **Fisher's Law #51.**

1. Control is necessary for good employee morale.

Since a good control system offers checks and balances within the organization, it encourages and supports honesty. At some time in your life, I am sure, you have been a member of a group in which it was discovered that something within the organization, be it a club, barracks, dormitory, office, plant, etc., turned up missing. Presumably stolen! You knew that you didn't do it, but no one else except the thief knew that you didn't do it, and you along with all the other group members were suspect. Why? Because there was no control system that definitely assigned responsibility. You know what a demoralizing and frustrating feeling it is to have the cloud of suspicion hanging over your head with no way to prove your innocence.

2. Any control system can be beaten.

Mechanical and electronic controls can be interrupted, paper controls can be doctored, and records can be duplicated. Computer controls can be bypassed or broken into, and visual control can be rendered impotent by collusion or payoff. There is a story about the department manager of a large organization who insisted that no subordinates could leave their desks at the end of the day unless their desktops were completely clear of the day's work. Not only that, but the manager would periodically inspect desk drawers just before closing to be sure that subordinates were not sitting on projects and simply stuffing work in the drawers in order to have a clean desktop. How's that for a control system? It was beaten easily. The subordinates simply placed all their work in the mail envelope for the intrafirm mail system fifteen minutes before quitting time, addressed the envelope to themselves, mailed it, thereby leaving their desktops clean and drawers relatively empty, and would receive their own work back through the house mail at eight-thirty the next morning. You see the point.

3. The control system should not cost more than the value of the loss it's designed to prevent.

The "cost" is not only a dollar cost, it also applies to time, space, and employee utilization. It makes no sense to design an elaborate and expensive control system to preclude the loss of a minuscule amount of money or merchandise. A manager once reprimanded an employee, "I think you are ignoring our control system," to which the employee replied, "Yes, but somebody has to get the work done." You can't afford to build an overhead to monitor a control system that is more cumbersome than the activity it surveys.

While these things may appear to be common sense, in organizational life common sense is not always that common. Just think for a moment—with all the bright people we have in our organizations, who supposedly have common sense, how do we get into so many dumb situations?

The bottom line is that while controls are essential, overcontrol can inhibit personal and systemic productivity.

33

INTERPERSONAL SKILLS OF SUCCESSFUL EXECUTIVES

Much has been written in modern management literature about the personal qualities and characteristics possessed by key executives that cause them to reach the pinnacle of success in their organizations and move that organization to greater heights. This fascination with the attributes ascribed to these men and women is born, in part, from the universal desire to identify the elements inherent in individuals that can lead to major accomplishment and success, so those elements can be cultivated in others when clues to their existence appear. I have observed and worked with a number of highly successful executives and have found five "people skills" common to all of them. Here they are, in no particular order of priority or intensity:

1. **Supportive of subordinates.** Successful executives don't emotionally abuse or bruise people with cynicism or sarcasm, take precipitous or whimsical actions that embarrass or reduce the stature of subordinates in the eyes of others, betray trust, or exercise unwarranted power that undercuts or retards the best interest of their subordinates, given the long-term best interest of the organization. Successful executives are supportive of people, possessing an ability to remember names and circumstances that are of personal importance to those under them. In this way, successful executives are considered thoughtful, caring people, not

just business automatons. They emphasize the positive traits and virtues of subordinates and frequently acknowledge the "team" nature of organizational endeavors without sounding like a paid corporate "cheerleader" or "PR person." They are able to evoke the maximum effort from subordinates by bonding performance to organizational loyalty. They "stand behind" as well as "stand with" subordinates.

2. **Delegates trust.** Successful executives have made the transition from being "hard-charging go-getters" in the individual sense to deliberate "thinker-planners" looking to the long-term future of their organizations, not just short-term expediencies. They recognized long ago that they had to stop "doing the work" themselves and had to "see that the work was done." Thus, they delegated, but they delegated trust along with authority and assignments, which subordinates perceived as an ordination of mutual commitment. In this way, successful executives are more than leaders of their organizations; they are statesmen and stateswomen of their industries and, often, of their communities.

3. **Balances control.** Successful executives do not overmanage by overcontrolling, overanalyzing, overreporting, and overcommunicating by overmeeting or causing overwork. They are effectiveness- and efficiency-minded to be sure, but they structure control systems to facilitate progress, not inhibit it. They are not encircled in their thinking by their own earlier experiences, and are not chained to the past by "tradition" or "custom" within their organization. They stress innovation and imbue this outlook in subordinates. They are open, not secretive, and stimulate and encourage contrary views in an atmosphere of respectful tolerance to be sure all views are expressed.

4. **Directness of approach.** Successful executives are very direct, not abrupt, in their relationships with others. This is necessary not only from a time-saving standpoint but from that of a sturdy organizational framework that comes from people "being up front," "knowing where I stand," and "knowing my voice is heard." It is the healthiest environment in which to thrive. Successful executives do not engage in or promote internal political

intrigue, or tolerate destructive rival factions within the organization. They are outspoken without being offensive, objectively critical without being caustic, future focused within the bounds of reality, measurement conscious without being inflexible, and understanding at the human level as well as the business level.

5. **A "sixth sense" about people.** Successful executives seem to have an innate ability to read people quickly and accurately, and, accordingly, surround themselves with other able persons possessing complementary talents with minimal conflicting or irritating traits. Successful executives give considerable free rein to their subordinates and don't "bash them to fit" preformed molds in an organizational cubicle. They have a strong awareness of self, but also have a keen awareness of subordinates and matters having impact, positively or negatively, on them. They portray for themselves, and demand of their subordinates: excellence, not excuses; self-esteem, not haughtiness; confidence, not arrogance; concern, not insensitivity; a progressive perspective, not blind ambition.

There are many other factors bearing on the "success" of successful executives, but people skills *are* the most important. Someone once said that eighty percent of successful management is getting along with people. I don't know if the number is right, but the thought certainly is.

Fisher's Law #52:

There is a strong, positive correlation between good people sense and good business cents!

34

PRODUCING PRODUCTIVITY PRODUCTIVELY

With tongue partly in cheek, let me express a thought on the subject of "productivity." It's a topic of increasing interest and concern, and I'll approach it using a metaphor. Definitions first, so we start from the same base. It's been stated frequently that there are three ways to increase productivity:

1. Maintain the same level of output with a reduced level of input.
2. Increase the level of output while maintaining the same level of input.
3. Increase the level of input slightly to yield a disproportionately larger level of output. This is often referred to as part of the economies-of-scale concept, or "leveraging."

There is a fourth possibility, but it's not always practical for business use. That would be to rapidly decrease input with a slower decrease in output so the "productivity margin" widens in the short run. This is usually self-defeating, however, unless it's part of a phase-out or a longer-term exit strategy.

So much for definitions. Note that inputs and outputs can be expressed in a number of ways, such as dollars made or saved, hours worked, customers served, products made, number of employees, or sales per employee.

Let's take a hypothetical case and apply a combination of these ideas. We'll use baseball as the example. That's right, baseball!

Baseball needs to be more productive. Solution number one: Have a pitcher and a catcher and no other fielders. You've just saved seven salaries. That's reduced input. The batters who come up to the plate would all be .300 hitters, if not .800 or .900 hitters, which would be good for the gate and baseball's statistics. That's increased output. Further productivity gains could be achieved by eliminating the catcher, since a resilient backstop could return the ball.

Don't like that solution? Okay. Here's another alternative. Solution number two: Keep nine people on the team, which maintains the same input, but expand the normal game to twelve innings and allow each team six outs in their half of the inning. That way there would be more turns at bat, more pitches, more fielding chances, more "big plays," which would result in increased output.

Don't like that one either, huh? All right, let me try solution number three: Put ten persons on a team and have four outs per half inning. That's slightly increased input. You can then expect many more runs, many more strikeouts, and many more customers, such as relatives and friends of the players. That results in greatly increased output.

Then there is always that usually impractical solution number four: Pack the ballpark and then cancel the game without refunding the tickets, or give rain checks that are good only on rainy days. That could save players' and groundskeepers' salaries, which will drastically cut input. With a widened "productivity margin"–remember, you didn't refund the money, the parking and food concessions would still operate, which is a slower decrease in output. Realize, of course, that this action wouldn't result in pure profit, since you'd have increased expenses for fan riot control, stadium repair, and press relations and crisis management seminars.

No, I don't have my foot in my mouth, but I do have my tongue partly in my cheek. You can see the patent absurdity of the foregoing proposals.

I thought I would use a little humor to emphasize **Fisher's Law #53.**

102

> Productivity is not only a numbers concept; it's also a value concept, a point that is too often overlooked. Quality, not quantity, must be the dominant feature in contemplating productivity increases and methods to achieve them. The most productive organizations are the ones that are the most value conscious.

Numbers are only numbers; you really need to look at the value effect behind them.

35

S.E.R.V.I.C.E.

It's time to express some thoughts about the concept of SERVICE, which some people in our society feel is declining.

SERVICE is receiving increased attention these days, as organizations attempt to gain or maintain a competitive edge in the marketplace. Survey after survey indicates the general public is critical of the services they receive, or perhaps do not receive, from retailers, public agencies, and other institutions with which they come into contact. At the same time, customers indicate they want better service and frequent those organizations where they believe they are getting a service value as well as a product value for their money. Since service is being touted as a point of competitive differentiation, it behooves us to take a look at it in terms of both its definition and its composition.

Everyone has a definition of "service" based on individual experiences. Service is often in the eyes and ears of the beholder. It may be hard to describe, but we know it when we experience it. Nevertheless, in order to establish a common base, I offer the following definition: "Service" is correctly anticipating the needs and/or desires of customers and customer prospects, and taking timely, appropriate action to fulfill or exceed those expectations to the complete satisfaction of the customers, resulting in the highest transaction exchange value possible and a positive predisposition for a continuing relationship in the future. I know that sounds terribly academic, but it's comprehensive, as it needs to be.

Now let's turn our attention to the elements of service. There are seven of them, embodied in the word itself.

1. **S**pirit is what is required in the people who will be performing the service. It all starts with spirit. You need to recruit positively spirited people to your organization, train them, retain them, and constantly nurture the service culture and service attitude that should abound throughout the entire system.

2. **E**mpathy is the ability of a service performer to place him- or herself in the mind-set of the customer so that the server can sense, through observation or telepathy, or both, the needs and/or desires of the customer. It's that "sixth sense" that needs to be operative, as anticipation is a necessary step in the service process.

3. **R**esponsiveness is taking timely and appropriate action to meet the expectations of the customers. Timeliness does not always mean being quick, for sometimes proper pacing is more important than speed. Appropriate action requires a balance so that goals are not underaccomplished nor are they overdone. A service performer should not "short-serve" a customer, be overbearing, or be excessively solicitous. Judgment is key.

4. **V**isibility of service is required, as the customer needs to feel that he or she is being served and that everyone in the entire environment knows that service acts are occurring. That's what gives an organization a pleasant "hum" of activity that makes people, both customers and service performers, glad they are a part of it.

5. **I**nventiveness is sometimes required to perform good service. It may be doing a little something extra, it may be overriding a system to resolve an unusual problem, or it may be following up on something at a later time. Your service performers need to be invention minded since everything they will encounter will not fit into predesigned service programs, packages, and policies.

6. **C**ompetency is essential for good service to be sustained and to thrive. The customer assumes competency on the part of the service performer, and if it is not evident, a disservice occurs that exacerbates a worsening situation. Service performers need to possess and exude gracious competency to initiate the server-customer relationship on a basis of mutual respect.

7. **E**nthusiasm is the crowning touch that service performers need to possess to maximize the transaction exchange value with the customer during the immediate interface. Soaring enthusiasm is good for everyone: the organization, the customer, and the server. It ties back closely to *Spirit,* which completes the service loop and causes customers to reflect well on their experience and want to come back.

Service is easy in concept but is more difficult in execution. **Always try to remember Fisher's Law #54:**

SERVICE equals PROFITS—People Returning Often For Insured Total Satisfaction.

36

DEFINING MOMENTS

There will be several instances in your professional life that will make an indelible mark on you and the way you progress through your career. They are defining moments, for the way in which you respond identifies your core being as a person, and the world will know "the stuff" of which you are made.

Allow me to present some issues that you are likely to face, as I want to provoke your thinking so you can be ready for them when they occur.

1. An employee has not been performing well and a termination is in order. Do you tell the employee that the cause of termination is a general reorganization, an overall reduction of personnel, or do you actually enumerate to the employee the elements of his or her performance that have led to the dismissal.

2. Your purchasing manager has dealt with Company A for a considerable period of time and has received good quality and good service. It's been a good relationship. A salesperson for Company B visits and can match Company A's quality, service, and price schedule. The Company B salesperson also indicates that Company B is holding a week-long seminar in two months for its major customers at a luxurious resort with spouses included. Your purchasing manager would be invited "once the order is placed." You become aware of the situation. Do you do anything? If so, what?

3. A job applicant from another city visits you for an interview. By happenstance, you learn that the applicant is also interviewing with other organizations in your area on this trip. The applicant

sends you the bill for the full cost of the trip, with copies of the air-fare stub, hotel bill, meals, and airport parking. What do you do?

4. A human resources department employee in charge of the company suggestion system receives an excellent suggestion that will benefit the company. The HR employee tells another employee about the suggestion and further tells that second employee how to change the suggestion just enough so it doesn't "look copied" and to backdate it, so the second employee will receive the cash award and recognition. You become aware of what's happened. How do you address it?

5. A loyal, long-standing organizational subordinate brings you an insignificant gift, say, a small desk ornament. You think nothing of it. Then it happens again a short while later, but it's a little larger gift this time and it's personal. How do you handle it?

6. You are traveling with a co-worker for the first time. The coworker seems to be a solid type. You complete your assignment in the faraway city late in the day. You will fly back the next day. You go out to dinner with the coworker, who then becomes an entirely different person and begins to do some things totally out of character and which are alien to your interest, values, and lifestyle. What do you do?

7. A co-worker in charge of production begins shaving two percent off the weight of a product and leaves out a minor and relatively insignificant ingredient that does not affect the safety of the product. These "shavings" are imperceptible to customers and there are no extraordinary complaints. Still, it's not up to established standards. The co-worker justifies such action as necessary to "make cost." How do you address this? Or do you address it? And to whom do you address it?

8. A large and important customer contacts you soliciting a contribution for an organization in which, while worthy, you have no particular interest or affiliation. The customer suggests an amount that is well beyond the scale of your capability. What do you say, and how, and in what environment do you say it?

9. A) A large, long-standing, and important supplier calls you

and indicates that a close relative is looking for work. You have never met the relative, nor do you know anything about the person. The supplier states, "I would consider it a personal favor and be mighty proud if my relative could be a part of your organization." You do have some positions open. How do you handle this?

B) Later that same day you get a call from a politician, say, the mayor of the city, who extols the virtues of your suppliers' relative. Thus, you become aware of the "political" connection. What do you say to the politician?

C) Assuming you meet with the supplier's relative, you will come to a decision. You will either hire the person or you won't. Assume you don't. What do you say to the applicant? Do you also communicate your decision to the supplier? If so, how do you handle it? Do you also communicate with the politician?

10. In a large meeting at which you are in attendance, the presider starts enthusiastically by speaking about a major accomplishment that has occurred in which unquestionably you played the major role. In the comments the presider mentions the name of one of your colleagues who was also involved, but only in a very minor way. The presider continues, incorrectly, to lavish praise on this person, and, inexplicably, your colleague begins to bask in the glow and says nothing. What do you do, if anything, and when do you do it, and how do you do it?

11. At an organizational social occasion at which males and females are present and at which some important outsiders are also in attendance, one of the attendees captures attention and proceeds to tell a decidedly off-color and graphic joke that contains foul language. What do you do if:
    a) The person is part of your organization.
    b) The person is one of the outside guests.

12. A long-term employee of average capability and performance all of a sudden hits the wall of nonproductivity. The problem does not appear to be health related, mental or physical, and as far as you know there is nothing amiss in the employee's personal life. You ask for the employee's personnel file folder. Surprisingly, you find that the employee just turned sixty-four. The

employee doesn't look it at all. Normal retirement age is sixty-five. What do you do?

13. You have a situation where you go out to bid on one of your contracts or agreements every three years. The bidding process will soon begin. On your birthday you receive a stunningly beautiful gift from the incumbent contractor, well beyond what even your own family members would give you. You don't know exactly, but you have a fair idea of the price range. Expensive! What do you do?

14. It has come to your attention that one of your organizational associates is engaged in "backbiting" and you are the target. It starts with half-truths and progresses to untruths; it starts personally, such as "dresses like it's the 1940s," and progresses to incompetency: "He/she's not really that good, all front and no substance." What do you do if the backbiter is:

a) A higher-level manager, but not your boss.

b) On the same organizational level as you are in your department.

c) Is a subordinate but in another department.

d) On the same organizational level as your are but in another department.

15. An inspector enters your premises, takes several notes, and cites multiple "violations" that are marginal at worst, are highly debatable, and/or can be rectified on the spot. The inspector states, "This is really a shame. I hate to have to do this. It's too bad there's not a way we can work it out. I'd like to be able to work it out in some way." The inspector looks at you expectantly for your response. How do you handle it?

16. A position becomes available to which you have long aspired. You are hands down the most qualified person to take the position, and most observers have the expectation it will fall to you. Inexplicably the offer is extended to another person, who accepts. What do you do? Resign? Castigate or undermine the other person? Deride the process? Deny your interest? Silently grit your teeth and continue what you are doing? Vow to have revenge?

Become an ardent supporter of the new person? Cease communication? Champion the organization all the more?

17. A steady and reliable customer pays down the current balance of your receivable. Two weeks later, a second check arrives in the same amount. There has been a duplicate payment. What do you do with the check? Return it? Deposit it? Write out your check and send it with a letter of explanation as to what it represents, that is, a refund of a duplicate payment? How quickly do you take the action you are going to take?

18. An organizational colleague with whom you have strained relations due to that person's embarrassing you or treating you badly in the past is in a serious predicament. You are in a position to measurably help that person. You know that, and the person also knows that. There has not been a request for your assistance. What are you doing to do? Let the person hang? Do nothing unless there is a request for your help? Refuse assistance? Volunteer support? Assist without anyone knowing it?

19. In the process of recruiting a senior-level executive to join your organization, you are a member of a committee that meets, greets, and dines with the recruit. Over a meal, in the zeal to woo the person to the organization, a colleague expounds about an aspect of the organization that you know is not true. What are you going to do?

20. A subordinate comes to you and somewhat sheepishly indicates that one of her peers, a male, is making conversation and comments that make her feel uncomfortable. Nothing blatant, direct, or overt, just certain phrases. She is reluctant to say she is being harassed; the word she keeps using is "uncomfortable." What is your next step?

21. You are part of a two-person project team. Your partner pleads a busy schedule, so you wind up doing most of the work. The finished product is in the hands of your team member and the panel to whom it is to be presented. At the presentation, your colleague seizes the moment and dominates the presentation. Your

colleague has mastered your work well and presents it accurately. At the conclusion, you both receive appropriate equal credit and "well dones." Do you say anything to anyone? To whom? When?

Well, I think you see the point. You will face these types of things with some frequency.

My purpose is to have you pre-think vexing situations and not go into them blindly. It may help if you always remember these two **Fisher's Laws:**

#55: You can never defend a wrong, but oftentimes what's right needs a lot of defense.

#56: Make any defining moment you encounter a fine moment.

37

MOTIVATORS

One of the enigmas of human interrelationships is how to best get other people to do exactly what you want them to do. Such interrelationships abound throughout all areas of human endeavor, but in this Fisher's Law we'll focus on employer/employee relationships.

Until somewhat recently there was a major debate in management circles as to whether a) one person could motivate others, or b) people can motivate only themselves, and a supervisor, for example, can influence only the conditions through which employees become motivated in and of their own accord. The issue is pretty well settled in favor of the latter, although some still argue that certain elements of a relationship, such as force or coercion, do not truly motivate people, it terrorizes them.

Nonetheless, there are approximately ten motivating factors that set the stage in which the behavior of people is influenced in the direction in which you want them to act. Insight and judgment are needed, however, as to what factor or combination thereof appeals to which people at any given point in time. That is the management challenge. Let's take a look at these sectors in no particular order.

1. **Idealism**–Some people are motivated by ideals that build on their personal value system, causing them to act in a manner that transcends everyday existence. The "call" to go above and beyond normal duties, to give extra or prolonged effort because it's the right thing to do, or the belief that one can reach higher personal and/or organizational fulfillment is a powerful motivating influence. If it's the "right" thing to do (values), most people will do it.

2. **Accomplishment**–Some people are excited when they see things being accomplished and they are a part of it. Trainers have long known that trainees should be given readily achievable tasks in the forepart of their training so that achievement can be self-recognized as a spur to continued development. Getting things done provides sustaining momentum.

3. **Teammating**–Some people have a strong need for affiliation, to be part of a larger group, as group maintenance elements are important to them (belonging, camaraderie). They seek and need acceptance, and the team, or group, with its structure and support systems, are bolstering to the individuals who comprise it. They act because they don't want to let the team down or be subject to the team's sanctions.

4. **Independence**–Other people, or sometimes the same people at other times, are motivated by the autonomy they enjoy. They like being held individually accountable, setting their own pace, functioning in their own style, and exercising their discretion. They perform best without close supervision or being engulfed by a bureaucratic maze.

5. **Fear**–This is a controversial element, but if you define "motivated" as behavioral acts undertaken irrespective of "willingness" or "cooperation," then fear has to be recognized as a powerful motivator. Fear can be intrapersonal (fear of embarrassment, for example) or interpersonal (intimidation by others, for example). Early fear can be positive at both levels, such as overcoming "stage fright" or becoming a "good soldier" after an experience with a tough "drill sergeant."

6. **Prestige**–Recognition factors stir some people to action in that they not only want to be connected with a first-class group, which in itself is prestigious, but their position within the group compels them to act in a certain way. A reputation of "never having missed a day of work" is motivational to a person who has, and is recognized as the reward for an unbroken attendance record.

7. **Rationality**–Logic plays a part in the performance and motivation of people. That's why it's important to have everyone see the

big picture, not just his or her own more limited sphere. If you are told, for example, that you are going to sell a product or a service at a financial loss (illogical unto itself), it becomes logical if you can see that the draw of the loss leader results in greater overall profit.

8. **Safety**–Coterminous with security, safety is a powerful motivator for many people. Not just physical safety, but emotional safety and comfort rank high with them. They have always done what they are now doing (or, at least, have been doing for a long time) and they are content with that. The older one gets (approaching retirement, for example), the larger conservatism looms, and radical changes or "upsets" are not always welcome.

9. **Compensation**–People like to be rewarded, and money certainly plays a part, but it is not the be-all and end-all for many employees. Other forms of compensation, such as a positive environment, benefits, awards, and customer compliments, all play an important part. Money is just a number above a certain lifestyle level for many people, and it's certainly not always the first, or only, motivator to affect behavior.

10. **Curiosity**–Motivation for some people is based on the intellectualization of solutions to problems and challenges that are presented to them. Their behavior is governed by wrestling with and overcoming obstacles that are set before them. System developers, for example, often state that it is the challenge that attracts them and drives their activities. Their motivation lies in the thrill of breaking new ground for something that has not been done before.

Fisher's Law #57:

Motivation is the prelude to action. It's also the sustainer of action.

38

BOSSES

As you progress in your career, you will be exposed to a number of bosses with various management styles, personalities, and perspectives. You may be wise to think of them in the same light as they think of themselves. I have assembled one hundred "virtues" of being a boss, which you may find interesting and perhaps a bit humorous, but they have a truthful edge. Here they are:

1. Bosses are never insensitive, they are just being objective.
2. Bosses are never egotistical, they just possess stratospheric self-esteem.
3. Bosses are never indecisive, they just weigh all the alternatives very, very carefully.
4. Bosses are never reckless, they're courageous.
5. Bosses never take a break, they just want to experience a change of pace.
6. Bosses never take a vacation, they do external market research.
7. Bosses never get angry, they become concerned.
8. Bosses are never volatile, they just have a broad range of emotions.
9. Bosses are never nitpicky, they are detail conscious.
10. Bosses are never wrong, they are given faulty or incomplete information.
11. Bosses are never late, they were just taking care of a little problem.
12. Bosses never relax, they are just contemplating the future from a different vantage point.

13. Bosses are never impatient, they just excel at time management.
14. Bosses are never critical, they are constructively helpful.
15. Bosses are never speechless, they are just weighing their words carefully.
16. Bosses never experience self-doubt, they are just reassessing the situation.
17. Bosses are never radical, they're creative.
18. Bosses are never flashy, they're stylish.
19. Bosses are never confused, they are just sorting out the facts.
20. Bosses are never rash, they're action oriented.
21. Bosses are never stingy, they're prudent.
22. Bosses never get nervous, they just have a high intensity level.
23. Bosses are never without an answer, they just approach matters by asking questions.
24. Bosses never register surprise, they register calculated spontaneity.
25. Bosses never leave early, they are on their way to a meeting.
26. Bosses are never frustrated, they are determined.
27. Bosses are never arrogant, they are self-confident.
28. Bosses are never whimsical, they have vision.
29. Bosses are never pessimistic, they are realistic.
30. Bosses are never unrealistic, they're optimistic.
31. Bosses are never skeptical, they're practical.
32. Bosses are never forgetful, they were just going to address the matter at a later time.
33. Bosses never lose self-control, they're just being dynamic.
34. Bosses never fail to be understanding, they understand only too well.
35. Bosses are never inconsistent, they're flexible.
36. Bosses never interrogate, they're just curious.
37. Bosses are never reclusive, they're just in a planning session.
38. Bosses never negotiate, they dictate.
39. Bosses don't get sick, they rest.
40. Bosses never preach, they teach.
41. Bosses never demand, they suggest.
42. Bosses never get in the way, they just want to be keep involved.
43. Bosses are never driven, they're motivated.

44. Bosses are never fierce, they're tenacious.

45. Bosses never work harder, they work smarter.

46. Bosses never become distracted, they're just generating different ideas.

47. Bosses never sleep, they meditate.

48. Bosses are never fixated, they're focused.

49. Bosses are never grouchy, they're resolute.

50. Bosses are never happy, they're temporarily satisfied.

51. Bosses are never slick, they're smooth.

52. Bosses don't just see things, they see through things.

53. Bosses don't just speak, they speak eloquently.

54. Bosses don't just hear what you are saying, they hear what you are not saying.

55. Bosses don't just feel, they absorb.

56. Bosses never pick up the check, they pick out the place.

57. Bosses never relegate, they delegate.

58. Bosses don't engage in gamesmanship, they engage in statesmanship or stateswomanship.

59. Bosses don't just write, they exude.

60. Bosses never exaggerate, they just show things in the best possible light.

61. Bosses don't study, as they are quick studies.

62. Bosses are never inattentive, they're preoccupied.

63. Bosses don't have idiosyncrasies, they have a management style.

64. Bosses are not rigid, they're consistent.

65. Bosses never retreat, they are just circling around another way.

66. Bosses are never speechless, they just realize that there is a time to speak and a time not to speak.

67. Bosses don't just stand behind subordinates, they also stand out front, leading them.

68. Bosses don't just speed-read, they speed-think.

69. Bosses don't just ingest information, they devour it.

70. Bosses never make errors, they have learning experiences.

71. Bosses never let someone (or something) get out of hand. They are just allowing a little more leash.

72. Bosses don't just do things right, they do the right things.

73. Bosses are never oblivious, they just choose to overlook it.

74. Bosses never hold a grudge, they just have long memories.
75. Bosses know when opportunity knocks, they don't knock the opportunities.
76. Bosses never overtalk their points, they're just completely thorough.
77. Bosses never undertalk their points, they just believe in brevity and letting the situation speak for itself.
78. Bosses never interrupt, they just want an immediate status report.
79. Bosses never get into a reactive mode, they are always in an active mode.
80. Bosses are never perplexed, they are just pausing until the right moment occurs.
81. Bosses never carry much money, but their associates do.
82. Bosses don't just think, they think big.
83. Bosses never wish, they make it happen.
84. Bosses never get ulcers, they give them.
85. Bosses never ask for help, they ask for teamwork and team think.
86. Bosses are never disorganized, they are just creative with work flows and communication patterns.
87. Bosses never have tight jaws, grit their teeth, or count to ten; they are just being strong in their restraint.
88. Bosses never make the same mistake twice, they are just reconfirming that history can repeat itself.
89. Bosses don't miscommunicate, others misunderstand.
90. Bosses are never stubborn, they just abide by unshakable principles.
91. Bosses are never sullen, they just have a lot on their mind.
92. Bosses are never nostalgic, they just keep referring to the past as a teaching tool for others.
93. Bosses never manipulate subordinates, they challenge them.
94. Bosses are never bossy, they are crisply direct.
95. Bosses never beat around the bush, they tell it like it is.
96. Nothing ever goes over the head of the boss, or else it comes out from under the feet of subordinates.
97. Bosses are never bored, they just need to take a deep breath now and then.

98. Bosses are never funny, they just have a different sense of humor.
99. Bosses don't set constraints, they just want things to go through channels.
100. Bosses never pass the buck, they just want more research done.

Depending on the level of one's perch, people see things from different points of view.

I'll wrap this discussion up with **Fisher's Law #58.**

Bosses are never exactly alike. Neither are they totally different.

39

THE 12 E'S

There are likely to be a number of "first days" in your organizational life where you will assemble your full staff or department heads to meet for the first time with you as their manager. That first meeting is critical, as your subordinates will form their impressions and perceptions of you. You need to set the conditions, pace, standards, and ethics you will demand of yourself, and, by extension, what you expect of your subordinate. Here are some thoughts you may want to consider as you develop your remarks. I call them the 12 E's.

1. **Enthusiasm**–We need to exude enthusiasm both in our persona and for our mission and objectives of our organization, in our function and in our tasks. Our enthusiasm can be contagious. If we are not enthusiastic, ennui can take hold in our organization and that can lead to mediocrity–or even decline.

2. **Energy**–I believe energy is closely aligned with enthusiasm, as it connotes movement, action, passion, and spirit. I have found that self-starters are usually strong finishers. Energy is the personal electric current we infuse into the workplace and marketplace.

3. **Excellence**–We will establish or exceed current standards of performance for ourselves in pursuit of overall organizational excellence. We will be politely but directly demanding of continuing professional and organizational improvement in search of perfection.

4. **Example**–Recognize that we are role models for our colleagues at all levels of the organization. Others look to us, wanting

to give us one of their most cherished possessions–their trust. We will never besmirch our credibility, for if we did we would lose the trust of subordinates and our customers, and once trust is gone, there really is nothing left.

5. **Empathy**–We will place humanitarianism well ahead of materialism, people before artifacts, values before judgments, thoughts before action, and reason before decisions. Accordingly, we have or will develop the ability to step outside our own minds and into the minds of others, thereby seeing and understanding their perspective, feeling their emotions, and relating to their activities.

6. **Effectiveness**–We know that what we do makes a difference. We will set or help set a direction toward an attainable and sustainable goal, and we will get results. Our work service and work product reflects our knowledge, our skills, our talents, and our creativity, all devoted to noticeable and measurable accomplishment.

7. **Efficiency**–We will maximize the most important commodity in our lives–time. We will also optimize our output, starting with the input and carefully managing the throughput. We will minimize waste, synergize resources, and symbolize dynamism.

8. **Empowerment**–As we each possess expertise at what we do, there is a certain power that attaches to our role and to our persona. We have the ability to empower others to do things–by delegation, by inspiration, or by direction. We will not abuse power, we will use it to serve others in fulfilling our organizational mission.

9. **Essentiality**–In our relationships with people we will apprise them by both word and action that we regard them as absolutely essential to the success of our organization. We will be highly oriented to our customers both external and internal, and we will inform our subordinates, regardless of their position, title, or level within the organizational hierarchy, that they are an integral part of the success of our organization. If they were not essential, they wouldn't be with us.

10. **Esteem**–We possess or will develop self-esteem and we will draw the esteem of others. As you know, esteem rests on the four

cornerstones of integrity, character, self-confidence, and self-respect. We will place our greatest satisfaction in self-measurement, conduct ourselves with poise and dignity, have a high quality of life competence, and will continue to develop our specific expertise.

11. **Equilibrium**–With all the stimuli that are directed to us, and all the stimuli we issue, we will maintain a stable balance in our intellectual, personal, professional, and physical life. We possess self-control and are in shape, unflappable, fair, rational, caring, alert, forward thinking, responsible, and determined.

12. **Education**–We value education and training, recognizing that development for us and our subordinates is a journey, not a destination; a lifelong process, not a one-time event; dynamic, not static. If anyone ever doubts the value of continuing education and training, then consider the cost of ignorance.

I urge you to always follow **Fisher's Law #59.**

Eternally Embrace Every Element of the 12 E's.

40

EUPHEMISTICALLY YOURS

I have found that when people write something about someone else, they are extremely careful and guarded in what they put on paper. Whether it's letters of recommendation, evaluations, or ratings, there is frequently a tendency to use euphemisms, which result in an unreal word picture of the person in question. When you've read enough of these things, you can begin to decipher what the intended meaning really is. Here are some descriptive words that have their own definition but may be employed by a writer to convey another meaning. You have to look at the full text to get the real view. I'll alternate between the male pronoun and female pronoun for balance.

1. She's self-assured could mean she has a constipated ego.
2. He's respectful could mean he thinks he knows how to impress people.
3. She's loquacious could mean she never shuts up.
4. He's a risk taker could mean he acts before he thinks.
5. She's kind could mean she's a soft touch.
6. He's laid back could mean they don't come any lazier.
7. She's patient could mean she's a schemer.
8. He's adaptable could mean he doesn't have any backbone.
9. She's organized could mean she's overly structured.
10. He's eager could mean he wades in where angels fear to tread.
11. She's neighborly could mean she never returns what she borrows.

12. He's charming could mean you better hold on to your wallet.
13. She's attractive could mean she's stuck on herself.
14. He's expressive could mean he gestures wildly.
15. She's cheerful could mean she's unrealistic.
16. He's popular could mean he knows the latest jokes.
17. She possesses self-control could mean she's uptight.
18. He's optimistic could mean he doesn't recognize facts.
19. She's deliberate could mean she's painfully slow.
20. He's obedient could mean he doesn't have a mind of his own.
21. She's humble could mean she plays that role to the hilt.
22. He's a good listener could mean he's always thinking of what he's going to say next.
23. She's trustworthy could mean she's naive.
24. He has character could mean he is a character.
25. She's a conformist could mean she doesn't do anything innovative.
26. He's tenacious could mean he's an overbearing nuisance.
27. She's receptive to new ideas could mean she doesn't have any ideas of her own.
28. He's independent could mean he's not politically astute.
29. She's a numbers-oriented person could mean she has no personality.
30. He's a people-oriented person could mean he doesn't know numbers.
31. She's logical could mean she can find a million reasons not to do something.
32. He's competitive could mean he doesn't play by the rules.
33. She's even-tempered could mean she doesn't make waves.
34. He's assertive could mean he's abrasively inflexible.
35. She's creative could mean she can have an idea a minute.
36. He commands respect could mean he's a martinet.
37. She's involved could mean she's nosy.
38. He's reliable could mean he goes with the flow.
39. She's a good communicator could mean she talks a lot.
40. He's very persuasive could mean he really talks a lot.
41. She's very direct could mean she tells it like she wants it to be.
42. He's self-disciplined could mean he never comes in early or stays late.

43. She follows policies and procedures could mean she can't see the forest for the trees.

44. He's goal oriented could mean he can't see the trees for the forest.

45. She writes well could mean she writes often, often, often . . .

46. He lends stability to the group could mean he's a dragging anchor.

47. She gets along well with others could mean they tolerate her.

48. He'll go the extra mile could mean he likes to travel.

49. She is exceptionally active could mean she doesn't return phone calls.

50. He looks for added responsibility could mean he's never in his office.

Well, by now you see the point. I'll sum it all up in **Fisher's Law #60.**

Take written descriptions of others with a grain of pepper.

41

D.I.V.E.R.S.I.T.Y.

Progressive organizations are focusing intently and resolutely on issues of diversity within the context of their employee complement, customer base, supplier relationships, and community involvement. Unequivocally, the nation and most localities are becoming more diverse day by day, a trend that will continue to accelerate. With a polyglot population, managements are addressing and (hopefully) mastering issues related to race, ethnicity, national origin, religion, age, gender, sexual preference, education, language, and disability. While volumes can be written on the subject of diversity, perhaps it will aid understanding of what it is (good business) and what it is not (affirmative action) if we look inside the word itself. We need to start with a definition of diversity as a management concept.

Within an organizational context, "diversity is the inclusion of people in the workforce representing varied racial, ethnic, and cultural heritages, the management of whom requires policies, procedures, practices, and applications that ensure training for proper job functioning, recognition of performance, and opportunity for professional and personal development commensurate with the vision, mission, and objectives of the organization." I realize that's a mouthful, but we need to be both comprehensive and precise. Now let's analyze DIVERSITY:

1. **D**emographics–Organizations need to be cognizant of the general population demographics within the area(s) in which they conduct their businesses. They need to match the profile of their workforce composition with the geographical demographic profile

and customer database. This "situation analysis" is the initial step in developing a diversity management system.

2. Inclusion–Top management needs to come to grips with, firmly resolve, and commit to establishing or enhancing a diversity management culture within every aspect of the organization. Inclusion, not exclusion, is the byword since diversity makes solid economic sense and reaches to the highest plane of human virtue.

3. Values–Organizational culture is predicated on organizational values. If one values the worth and inherent dignity of individuals inclusive of the distinguishing characteristics, talents, and customs that comprise a segment of society, then one can recognize the benefit and celebrate the diversity that exists between and among different groups of people.

4. Engagement–Given demographics, a resolution for inclusion, and supportive organizational values, the next step is the engagement of people, both employees (recruiting) and customers (marketing), from diverse backgrounds. The diversity "bit" is now in your organizational "teeth" (to use an equestrian metaphor), and you're under way with a diversity management system.

5. Responsibility–The responsibility for successful diversity management is both organizationally wide and organizationally deep. It starts at the highest level, cascades throughout the entire management and nonmanagement structure, extends to the newest hire and the most recent customer, is perpetual and self-fortifying. It's accomplished through orientation, training, mentorship, marketing, reinforcing communications, and constant attention. Both successes and disappointments will occur, as with any aspect of life, but it is systemwide in its reach, implementation, and effectiveness.

6. Structure–The management of any organization, program, process, or procedure needs a structure, and the diversity dynamic is no different. Diversity can be managed, and therefore it should be managed in support of the organizational vision, mission statement, and stated objectives. Diversity management is one of the pillars of organizational structure just as are financial management, sales management, quality control, and facility management.

7. Identification–Once in place, and based on the preceding building blocks, the organization's various "publics" (employees, customers, the general marketplace, government, educators, suppliers, et al.) will identify the organization as a leader on the cutting edge of progress. Nothing succeeds like success, and that kind of momentum is contagious. In the reverse, nothing fails like failure, and failure is the seedbed for mediocrity or disintegration.

8. Tolerance–No road in life is without its potholes, no sea in life is without its storms. Diversity doesn't lead to Valhalla or Nirvana. If the support mechanisms are in place, however, coupled with the earlier stated resolve for inclusion and inculcation of values, then the "bumps" and the "waves" can be overcome. Tolerance and the appreciation of diversity are the indisputable qualities upon which organizational and societal progress rests.

9. Yield–At the end of the day, on the bottom line, when all is said and done, when the results are in, the final measure is the positive yield that is drawn from diversity. Measurement can occur over several dimensions: financial, morale, customer satisfaction, image, growth, and on and on. The yield will be decidedly better in the long run by embracing diversity management rather than ignoring it or resisting it.

Fisher's Law #61:

Gladly manage the diversity dynamic or you will be sadly outmanaged by your competition.

42

ALL-STAR TEAM

I've always felt that football is a recreational counterpart to an organizational environment, and I developed an allegory that compares football positions with organizational positions. I put the organizational terms in parentheses. Consider the following positions:

Quarterback (chief executive officer) is the keystone and pivotal position that determines all movement. The incumbent must have the game plan (vision and strategy) in mind well ahead of time (planning). The quarterback must be able to communicate clearly and issue forcefully the signals (directions) upon which activity will commence, so that all team members, even wide receivers (branches) and linemen (lower echelons), can hear them. The quarterback must command the confidence and respect of teammates (employees), the opposition (competitors), and fans (customers). On the quarterback's shoulders rests the responsibility to score (achieve goals) and win (succeed). Quarterbacks have to be able to read the defense (the marketplace and competitors), be alert (quick-minded) to blitzes (surprise thrusts by competitors), and adjust by calling audibles (altering strategy in light of changed circumstances). They must be able to hand off (delegate), lateral (refer to staff), stay in the pocket (office) when necessary, scramble (visit the field) when required, and pass accurately (defer to others) when necessary or desirable. If they fumble (drop the ball) or are intercepted (miscalculate), they could be replaced. They must learn to play with pain (pressure), be eternally resilient (vibrant), and keep their team working together (coordinated) as a team (organization). They have to have clear vision (foresight) and natural ability (competency). They must call the right mix of plays (marketing/financial strategy) and utilize their personnel properly (select carefully and assess performance).

Running backs (operating officers) must be able to take the handoff (directions) and advance the ball (programs) toward the end zone (company goals). They must be sure-handed (have a good grip on matters) and not be prone to fumbling (committing errors). They have to be both strong (forceful) to pick up the short yardage (break through barriers) and nifty (finesse) to slash (dart) through openings. They can't run off on their own (disrupt the system), and they have blocking responsibilities (mutual assistance). They must function as receivers (take assignments) when necessary.

Wide receivers (field force) must be swift (quick mental reflexes), as they are constantly in the defensive backfield (competitive marketplace). They must be able to report back (communicate) to the quarterback (CEO) what they think will work (suggestions) against the defense (competitive marketplace) when they return to the huddle (staff meetings). They must also be sure-handed (grip of the situation) as they receive passes (assignments) from the quarterback (CEO). They have definite routes (policies) and patterns (procedures) to run (follow), and must adhere to them (orderliness and discipline).

Offensive line (line personnel) are people who are in the trenches (on the firing line) and pave the way for progress on a consistent basis. They must be quick off the ball (on the ball) and be rugged (able to "take it"). Every responsible quarterback (CEO) knows he or she would be sacked quickly (out) if it weren't for the linemen (line personnel). There is little glamour and publicity (public recognition), but morale must be good (sense of pride) at all times. If one falters (misses), others have to double up (cover). They must be able to take signals (direction) and execute (perform) the play (according to plan).

Head coach (chairman of the board) is available to the quarterback (CEO) for consultation at critical points. The coach receives reports from scouts (bankers, consultants) on the opposition (competitive marketplace). The coach reviews play selection (plans) of the quarterback (CEO) and assesses performance and may even send in plays (plans).

Assistant coaches (board members) provide counsel and advice in areas in which they specialize. Along with the head coach (chairman), they comprise the coaching staff (the board). They may not have any execution responsibilities (outside directors) or may be player coaches (inside directors).

Fans (customers) are often volatile and fickle. They pay their money and demand performance. They may not support the team (buy product or service) if expectations are not met with satisfaction, or may switch allegiance to another (competitor) team (organization) if your performance is sloppy and you lose often. When you're winning (performing well), they can be great supporters (frequent customers) and make you the topic of conversation (word-of-mouth advertising).

Well, there you have it. There are, of course, some differences between a football team and your team–I mean your organization. Your people are not just Saturday's heroes or Sunday's heroes, they are everyday's heroes and heroines. Allow me to kick off **Fisher's Law #62.**

You have to let your people know constantly that in your eyes they are your all-stars. If you don't, you could get sacked.

43

RECRUITING THE BEST

A great measure of your success will depend on the type of people with whom you surround yourself, that is to say, those people you recruit to come work with you. Let's talk about the type of organization you want to run. Remember, we earlier determined that an "organization" is a system of interrelationships between and among *people*.

Some organizations are grossly inefficient and operate with limited, if any, effectiveness, which is readily apparent to the discerning eye. They are disorganized, which is worse than being unorganized. They exhibit an overall management sloppiness, slovenliness, lethargy, and laxity. Other organizations convey an immediate rigidity, a sterile and distant atmosphere, a robotized procession of people mechanically performing their tasks, lacking spirit, zeal, and humor, and clothed with an overabundance of restrictive controls and narrow procedural channels to accomplish their objectives. An organizational laxative would help them.

You should strive for your organization to emit an instantaneous receptivity, not only to visitors, but employee to employee, which translates into an interwoven vibrance allowing for goal attainment assuredly and consistently. It's interesting to note the common elements that underlie the success of these progressive firms—success defined in both economic and human terms.

1. In recruiting and selecting key management personnel, successful executives choose the most qualified, competent, experienced or trainable, intellectually versatile, multitalented people they can identify. They choose people who can do a lot of things

well. As a result, they run lean in terms of number of staff. This aids productivity, of course. Their organizational strength is in their breadth of talent, not depth of staff. They offer top salaries, believing that this is the best investment they can make. Since their strength is not quantity but quality, their overall payroll is still in line. For these firms, the phrase "catch the brightest stars" is more than an old reworked TV network slogan. The chief executive knows that hiring top talent is not a management panacea that will allow the reduction of managerial responsibility and time input. The management of highly spirited, multitalented people presents its own set of requirements for the CEO to master, but when the resources are there, the CEO has something with which to work.

2. Dynamic CEO's know that if the organization is to move forward, it's got to move up and move on. There is no room for the timid, the unsure, the "avoid all risks" type in progressive organizations. This is not to say that there is recklessness, whimsy, or irresponsibility aborning, that caution is thrown to the wind, or that mistakes are not made. It is to say that given deliberate and careful planning, with attention focused on both short-term tactical and long-term strategic objectives, there is a pragmatic boldness, controlled aggressiveness, and quiet confidence that pervades the organization, which assists in meeting and overcoming the risks incurred.

3. It often has been suggested that good executives work smarter, not harder. That's only partly true. Top executives are smarter, which *causes* them to work harder toward mastery of the established objectives. As objectives expand in scope and magnitude, the successful executive works harder, gaining in expertise and advancing the organization. This process allows people to become more knowledgeable, which in turn allows them to work smarter. There is an ascending self-reinforcing cycle of equal portions of keen intellect and physical effort that characterizes the employee force. An atmosphere of contribution to the organization exists among the employees. They give 110 percent of themselves, which in itself is a source of pride to them. They truly manifest the work ethic. In less successful organizations the atmosphere

exuded by employees is often in the vein of "I'll put forth the minimum effort; this place owes me something."

4. A central principle that is evident to the naked eye in successful organizations is the acceptance of decisions, by top management, which are made at the level of impact where the decision will be felt, consistent with the overall mission and operating and administrative policies. Organizational superiors don't normally reverse decisions of subordinates when they have delegated authority to those subordinates for those types of decisions. Consequently, there is considerable dialogue and a noticeable absence of monologue. Differences of opinion are not looked upon as one person or group being right and the others wrong, but as a matter of preference, or as arriving at different logical conclusions based on individual perception of the same set of facts and conditions. Decisions are made and directions chosen, to be sure, but there is no individual or departmental destructive rivalry, ego strife, or "upmanship" at play. Mutual trust, confidence, respect, and dedication among all employees is more than a byword in an orientation leaflet. It's practiced, and it's perfected.

I think you see the point, so let me wrap up this discussion with **Fisher's Law #63.**

The difference between serving people and processing people is sincerity. This applies to customers and employees alike. Recruit the best employees and you'll recruit the best customers!

44

THE MANAGEMENT OF TOMORROW

Those of us who are in the sunset of our years look with hope to those of you who are at the dawn of your careers. You have limitless opportunity and potential kindled by your own vision and ambition.

There will always be the unknown, but let me tell you what I see for generations to come.

Sense of Significant Purpose. Today's young managers seem to be happiest in an environment in which they have a sense of significant and measurable contribution to the known and constantly reinforced purpose of the organization, and of their role in reaching that purpose. Your scope of personal concern encompasses not only your own and your organization's welfare, but also the condition of society at large. You are more aware of national and world conditions than was true in the past. The world is not getting smaller; you have an expanded awareness.

You want to feel not only that your working life is contributing to the organizational purpose, but that the organizational purpose itself is upstanding. In terms of contribution to the betterment of society, you want us to be on the leading edge because what we do is socially useful, economically developmental, and personally fulfilling. You want to be professional, and you want your organization to be professional. You are likely to ask "Where can I contribute most?" rather than "What have you got to offer me?"

Growth Orientation. Young managers are most excited in an organization that has a growth perspective in terms of both accelerated penetration into existing markets and the attraction of new markets and projects. What is interesting, however, is that this appeal is not only based on your potential advancement, which is assumed to some degree, but of equal importance is your enjoyment of the growth dynamics of setting direction, assembling resources, deploying resources according to plan, measuring progress, and achieving goals. You want to squeeze in as much experience in as short a time frame as possible. In a growth-oriented organization, promotion and financial advancement are taken somewhat for granted, and, therefore, young managers focus on operational challenges and the mental stimulation that accompanies them. You want to have faith in us but sometimes feel thwarted and isolated, not realizing that others have the same pressures and problems. Some of us seniors apparently don't do a very good job of "post-sale marketing" with our employees. The growth perspective is based on a solid financial underpinning and you want us to be an organization of substance. Young managers are drivers and strivers, aggressive and progressive, conscientious and unpretentious, energetic and kinetic. You are confident, curious, trusting, optimistic, and analytical. You also know you have a lot to learn and you are simultaneously eager and impatient. You could also be more creative.

Customer Perspective. Young managers derive as much satisfaction from serving customers as they do from making budget and return on investment (ROI), although they worry that this is heresy to many of us. You are people oriented, and represent the wave of youth who are revitalizing the service ethic. Generally speaking, you don't have the servitude hangup that was evident some years back or is characteristic of those who are insecure. You delight in serving people, believing that it is the *right* thing to do. In this regard you have a generalized unselfishness. You are genuine, cordial, and sincere in your relations with others. You are also somewhat naive, however, having grown up in an abundant environment. You really haven't tasted failure, and scarcity hasn't touched you. Inflation is viewed as relative, and is something you read about. You tend to be overly trusting.

Positive Internal Climate. Another thread in the emerging management fabric is the desire of young managers to operate in a positive internal climate, wherein your thoughts are not disrespected because of your age, and you are not suspected because of your education. You like to be judged on performance, not seniority, be given responsibility, not assigned only minor tasks. You need reminding from time to time that you are a definite resource to the organization and want to feel that we provide a measure of loyalty to you equal to what you give to us. You want to be more than just on the team. You want to be in the game. You also want us to recognize that you want to live a quality life in all that you do.

Principles, Ethics, and Quality. Young managers are mindful of good business practices, organizational codes of ethics, and the quality level of the product and/or service of the organization. You are repulsed by violations in the name of expediency and short-term profit and recoil at decisions that are made on a nonobjective basis. You have a longer-term view as well as a global view, and seek solid answers to valid questions beyond "it's company policy." You have a social security number, an employee identification number, a driver's license number, a license plate number, a telephone number, several credit card numbers, and perhaps a locker number. You also have some flesh, some blood, and a mind you want to use. You think of yourself as a quality person who has something to offer, and you want to work with quality and provide quality in everything you do. You want to prepare for the future and need to feel you are *being prepared* for the future. You want to believe that the best of everything you will ever know is still ahead of you.

Let me sum up, as it's time for **Fisher's Law #64.**

The management of tomorrow will be only as good as the management of today allows it to be.

45

THE PERFECT EXECUTIVE

Well, I hope you have found these Fisher's Laws to be insightful and enjoyable, provocative and illuminating, revealing and elucidating.

I also hope you feel our time together has been beneficial, but I feel the need to come to complete closure to give you takeaway value for the investment of time you've made reading this book. Let me tell you about "the perfect executive" now that you are aware of all we have discussed.

First of all, we need to recognize that perfection is a value, not an object. Therefore, it's not wholly measurable quantitatively. Most of us recognize it, however, when we experience it. Here are sixty qualities that I feel are the components of the perfect executive.

The perfect executive possesses the following:

1. the *curiosity* of a cat
2. the *tenacity* of a bulldog
3. the *pride* of a peacock
4. the *humility* of a monk
5. the *eagerness* of a student
6. the *wisdom* of a professor
7. the *hope* of an optimist
8. the *courage* of a champion
9. the *dynamism* of a perpetual-motion machine
10. the *patience* of Job

11. the *memory* of an elephant
12. the *understanding* of a parent
13. the *skin* of a rhinoceros
14. the *sensitivity* of a teenager
15. the *discipline* of a ballerina
16. the *adaptability* of a chameleon
17. the *work ethic* of a beaver
18. the *service ethic* of a cleric
19. the *endurance* of a long-distance runner
20. the *pace* of a sprinter
21. the *thriftiness* of a Scotchsman
22. the *generosity* of a benefactor
23. the *poise* of a diplomat
24. the *perspective* of a statesman or stateswoman
25. the *vision* of a builder
26. the *confidence* of an achiever
27. the *respect* of a queen bee
28. the *sense of humor* of a comic
29. the *organizational ability* of a spider
30. the *creativity* of an artist
31. the *dedication* of an Olympic athlete
32. the *trust* of a friend
33. the *persuasiveness* of an automobile salesperson
34. the *inspiration* of a coach
35. the *resiliency* of a rubber ball
36. the *stability* of the Rock of Gibraltar
37. the *judgment* of an umpire
38. the *ambition* of an ant
39. the *integrity* of a judge
40. the *objectivity* of a scientist
41. the *motivation* of a treasure hunter
42. the *alertness* of a fox
43. the *analytical ability* of a computer
44. the *communication ability* of a crusader
45. the *standards* of a university president
46. the *goal orientation* of a hockey player
47. the *reliability* of a tax assessor
48. the *heart* of a lion

49. the *intellect* of Socrates
50. the *focus* of a jeweler
51. the *speaking ability* of a champion debater
52. the *writing ability* of a Pulitzer-prize winner
53. the *listening ability* of a psychiatrist
54. the *resolve* of a medical researcher
55. the *mental strength* of tempered steel
56. the *growth orientation* of a landscaper
57. the *enthusiasm* of a cheerleader
58. the *logic* of a mathematician
59. the *luck* of a lottery winner
60. the *spirit* of a person of accomplishment

And so, my friend, **Fisher's Law #65:**

The perfect executive is _____

**(Fill in your name, at the appropriate point
in your managerial maturity.)**

INDEX

Index

ABOUT THE AUTHOR

William P. Fisher is the president and chief executive officer of the American Hotel and Motel Association, based in Washington, D.C., a position he has held since 1996. Prior experience includes seventeen years as the chief staff officer for the National Restaurant Association, seven years as chief financial and administrative officer for a food management contract services organization, and more than four years as an assistant professor at Cornell University.

Mr. Fisher has also been a business consultant (simultaneously with teaching assignments), and is a former United States Air Force officer.

He holds B.S., M.B.A., and Ph.D. degrees from Cornell University.

He and his wife of thirty-five years have three children and four grandchildren, and are counting.

Mr. Fisher states he likes "WRITING ABOUT MANAGEMENT MATTERS AS LOUDLY AS I CAN."